contents

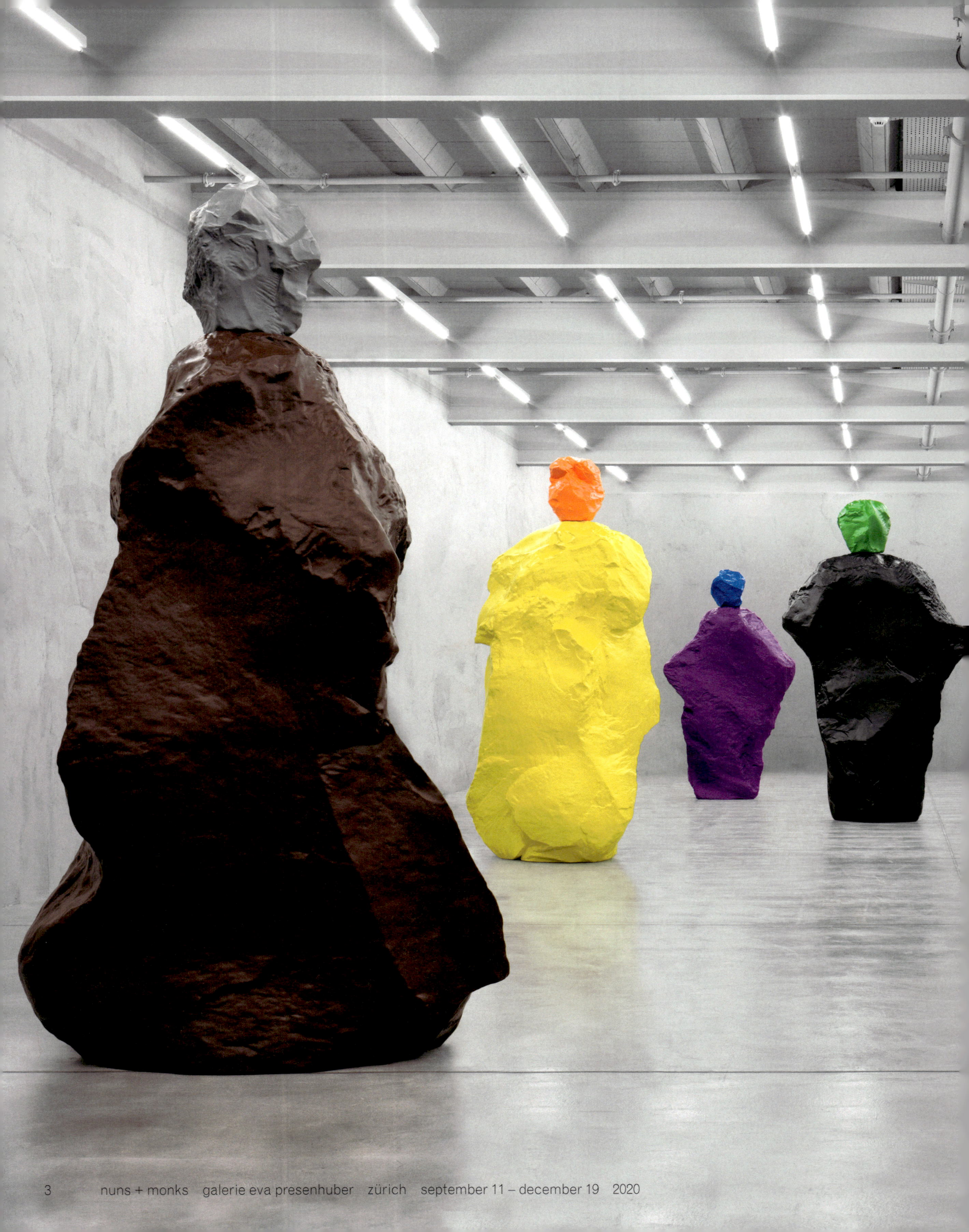

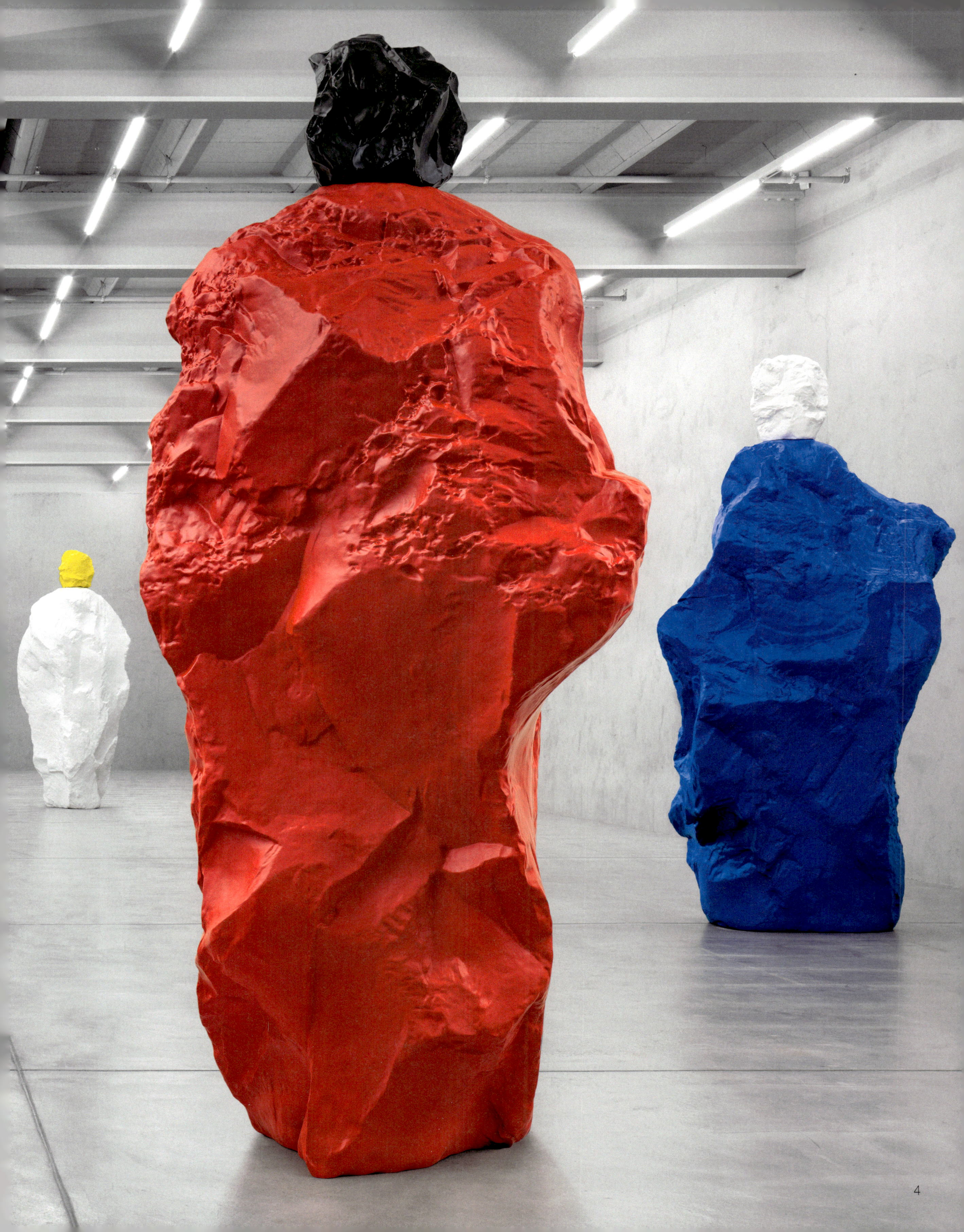

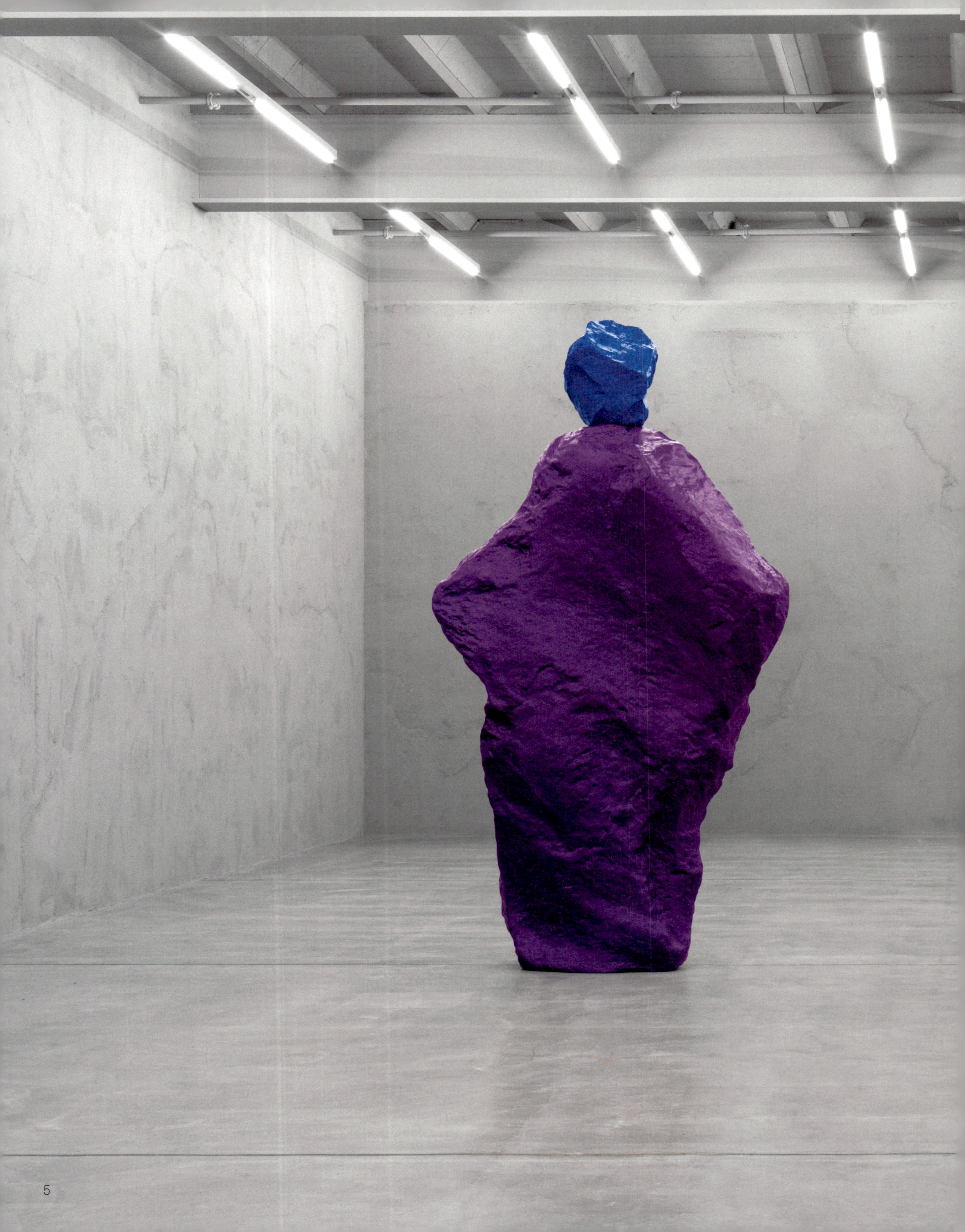

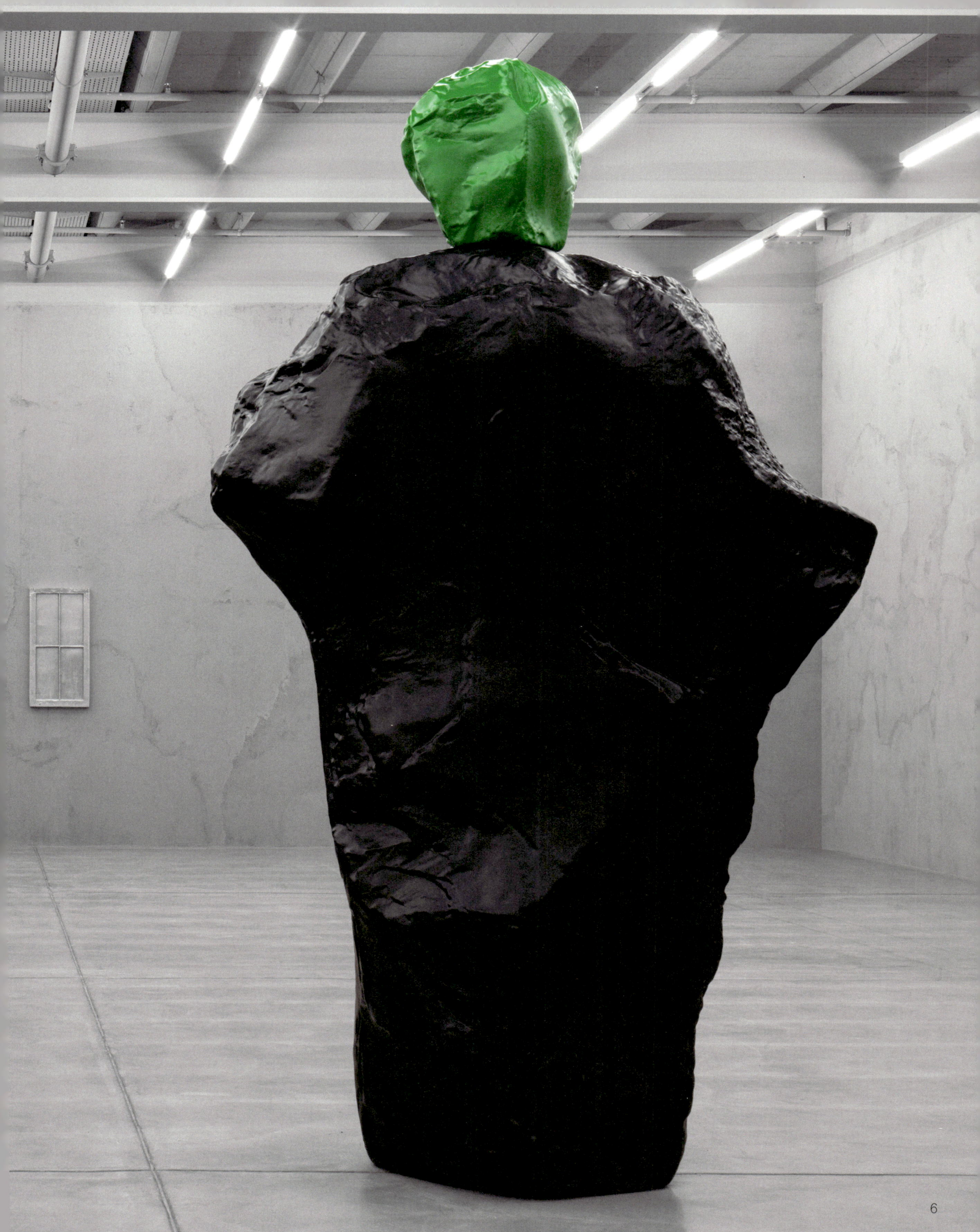

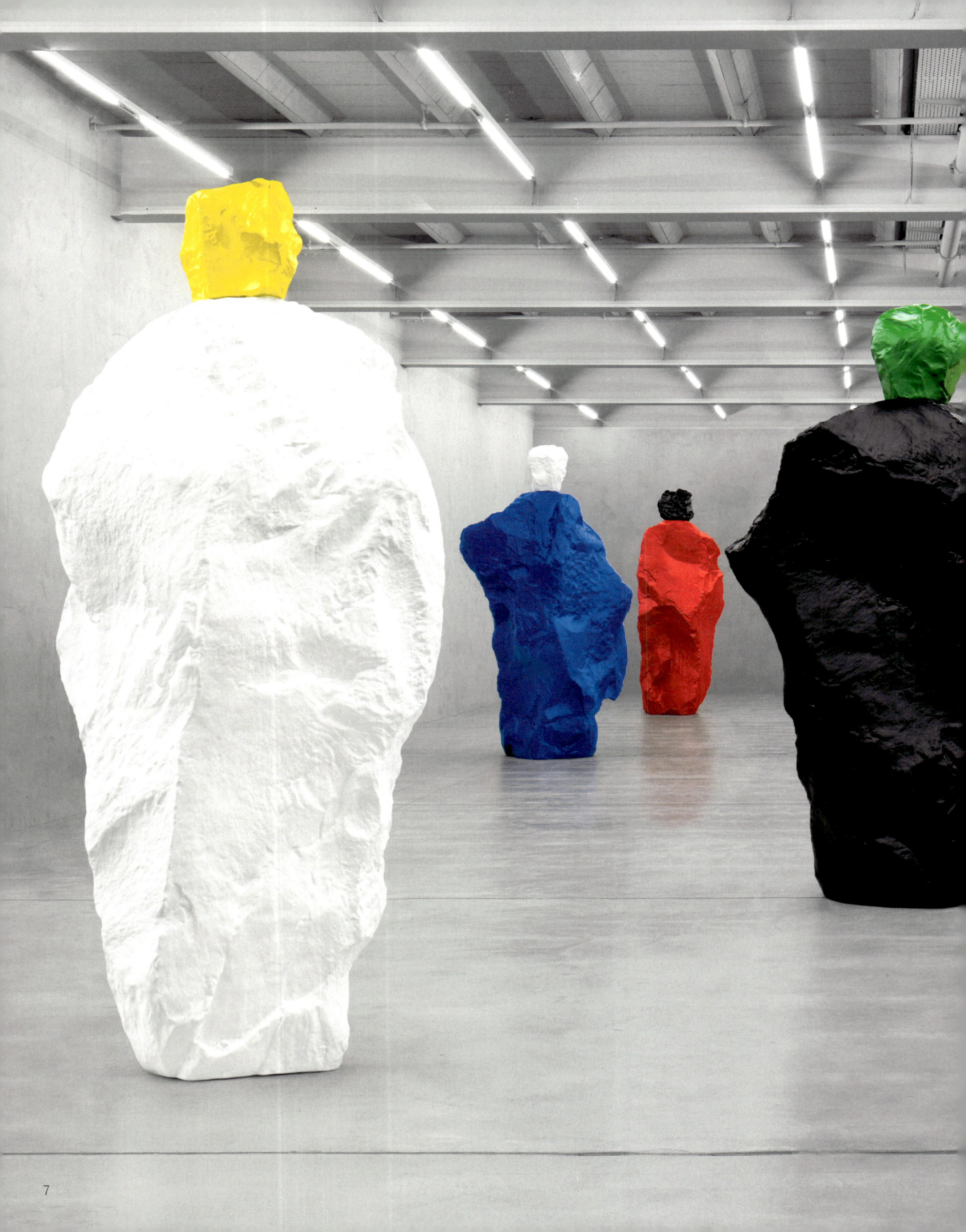

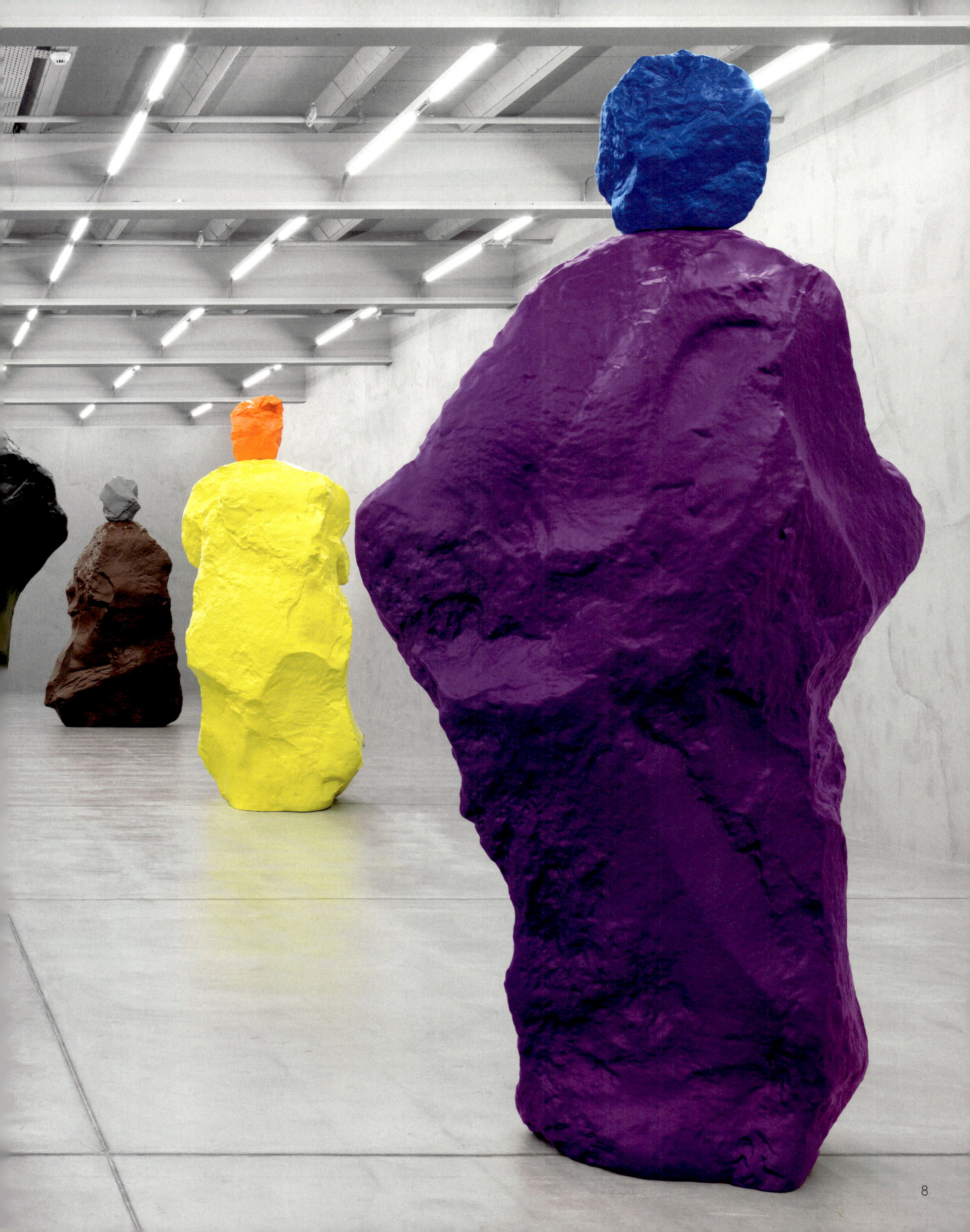

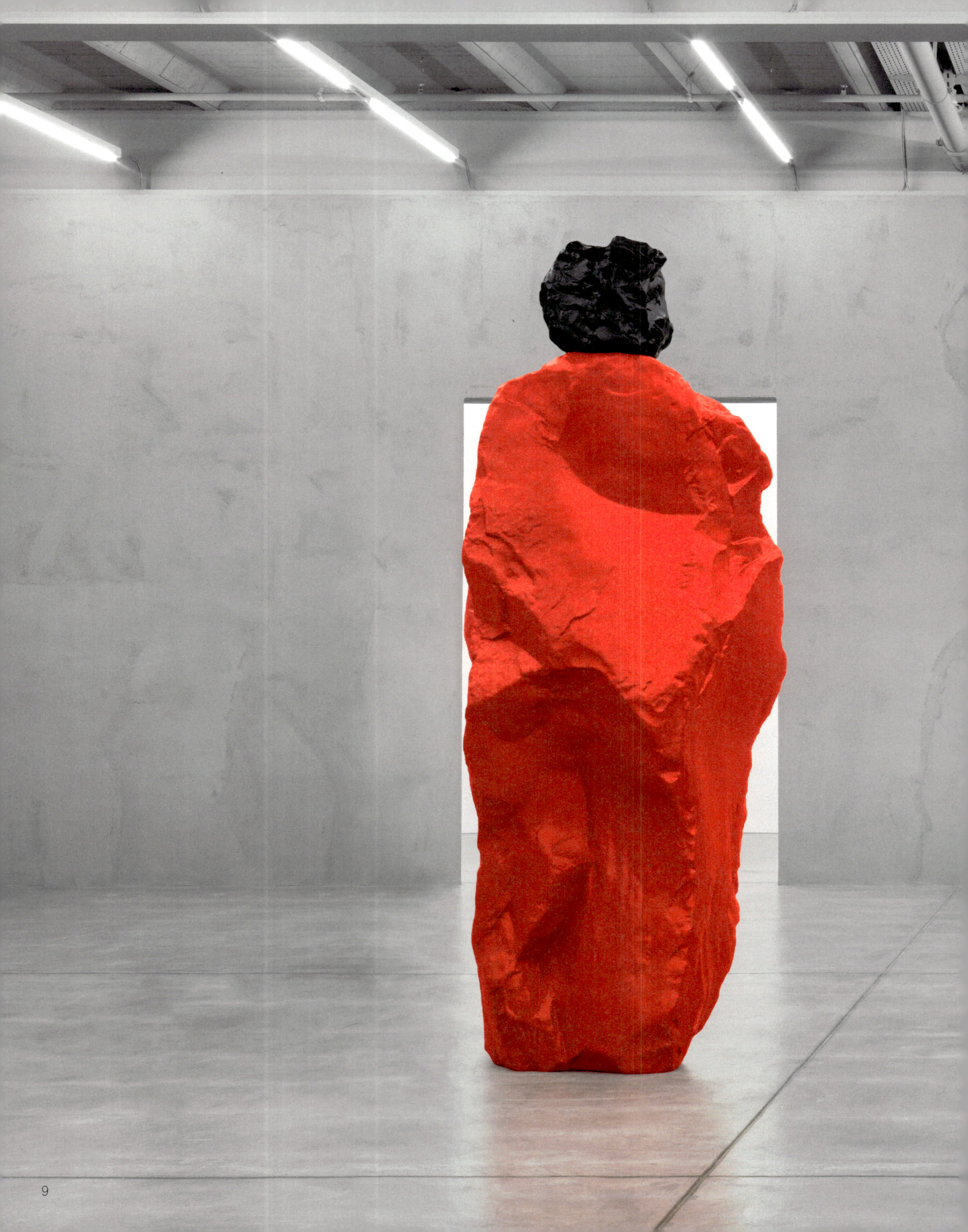

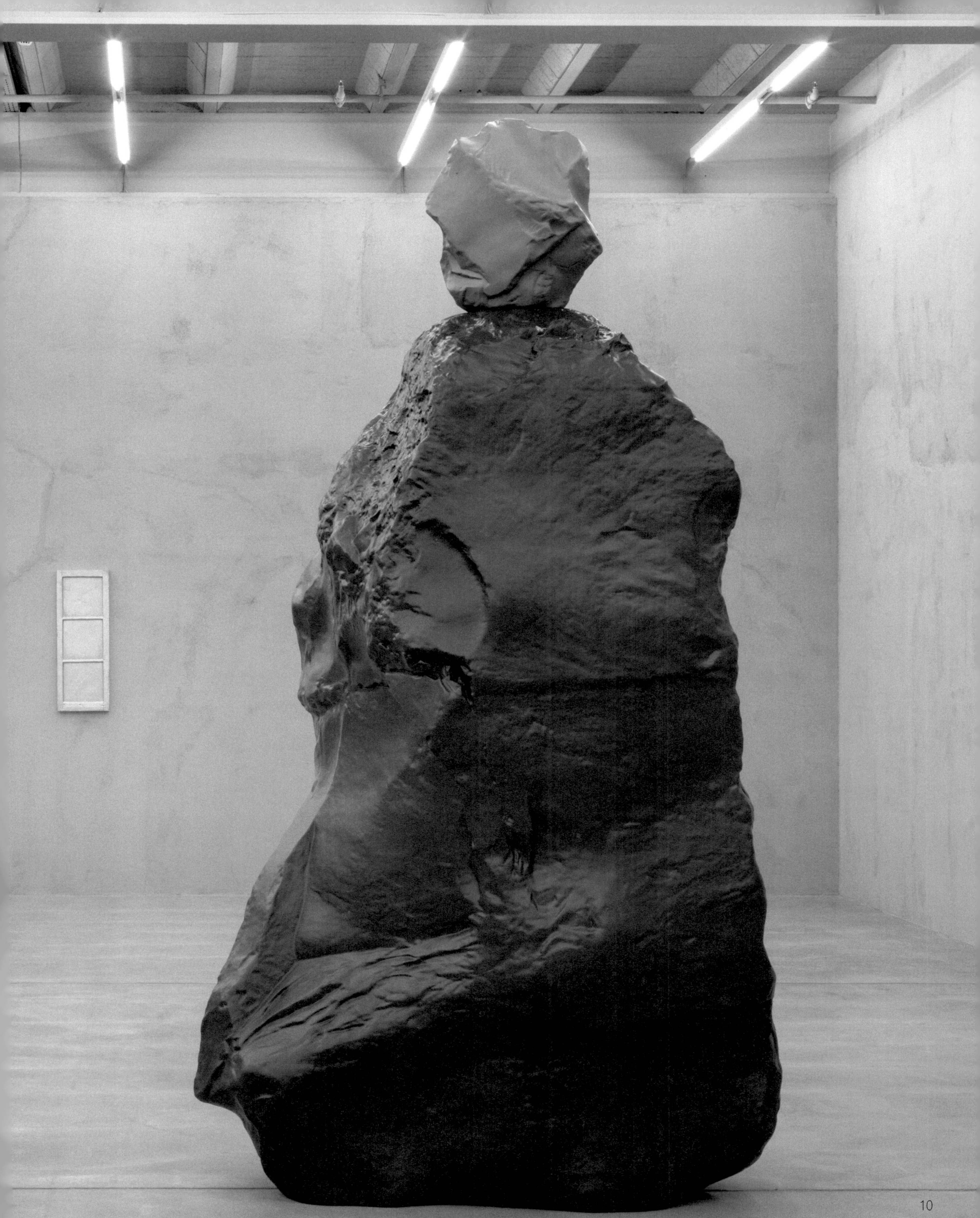

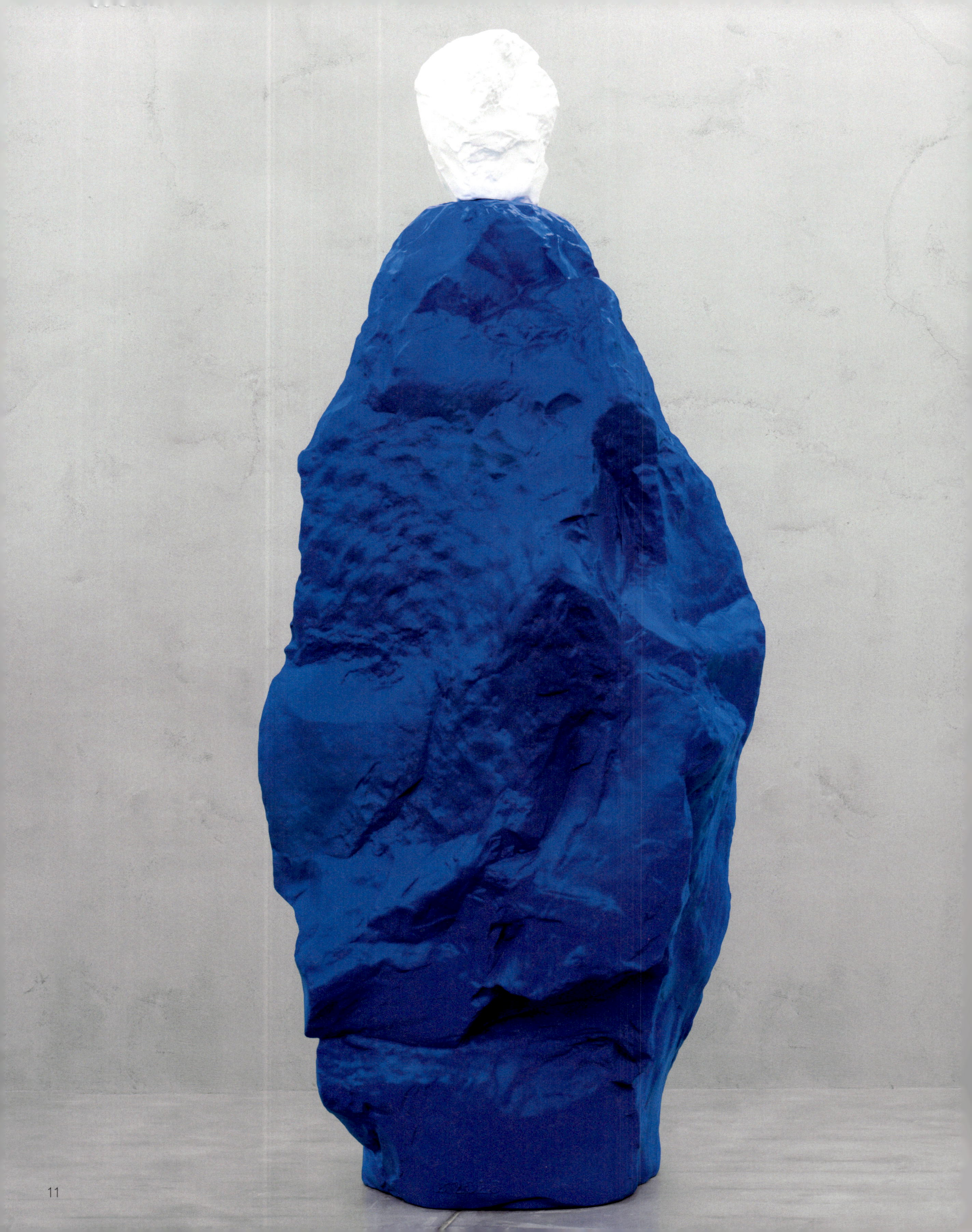

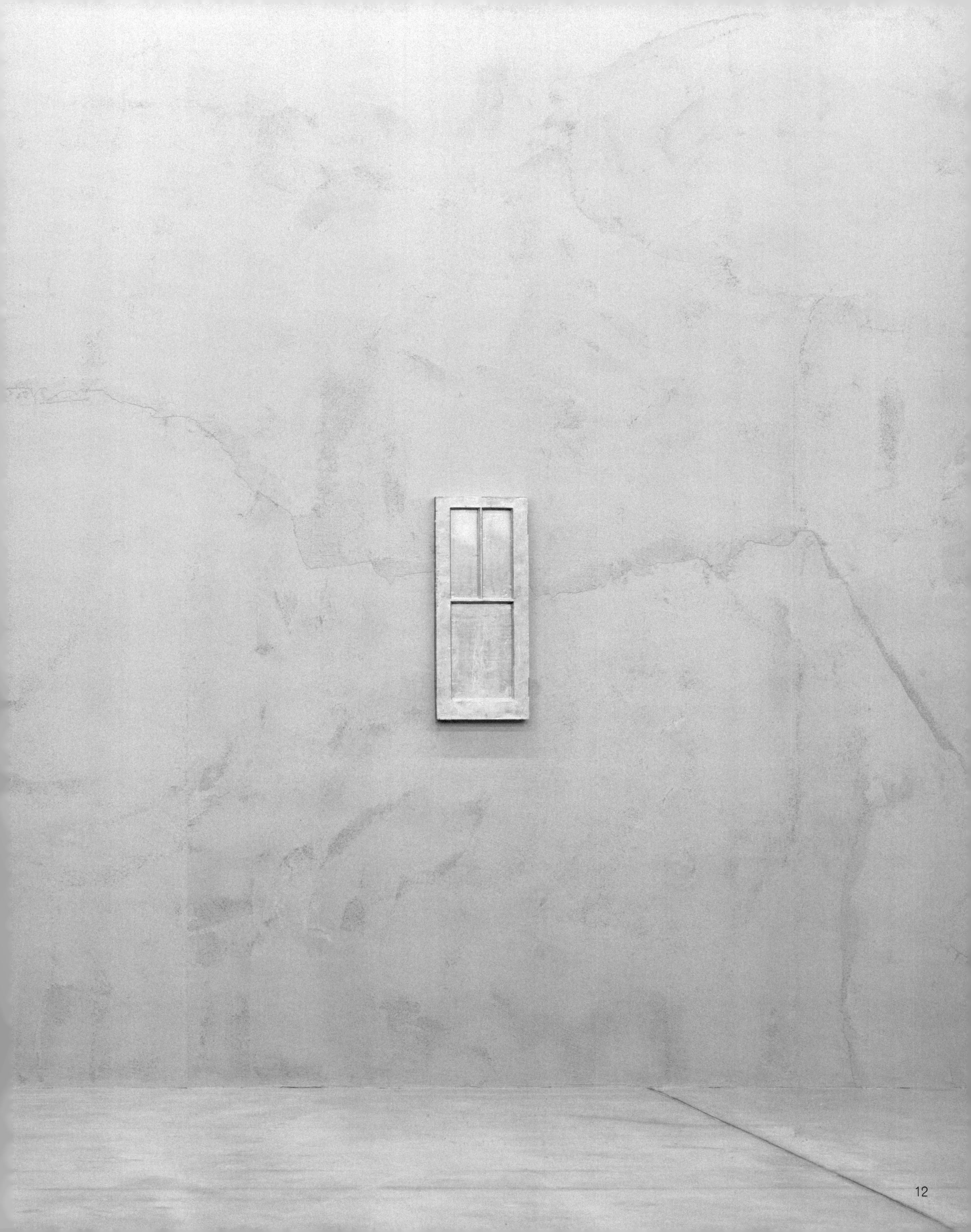

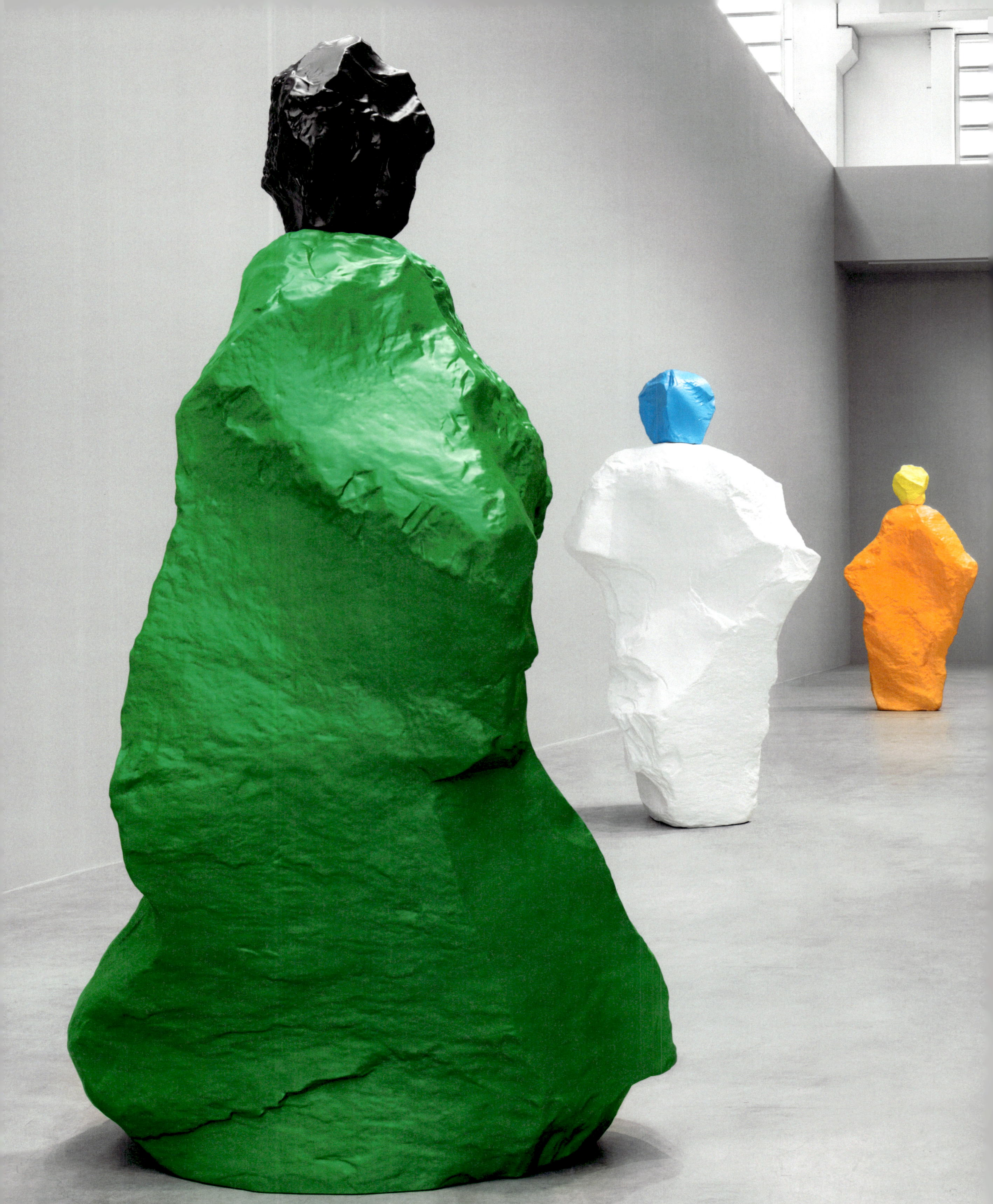

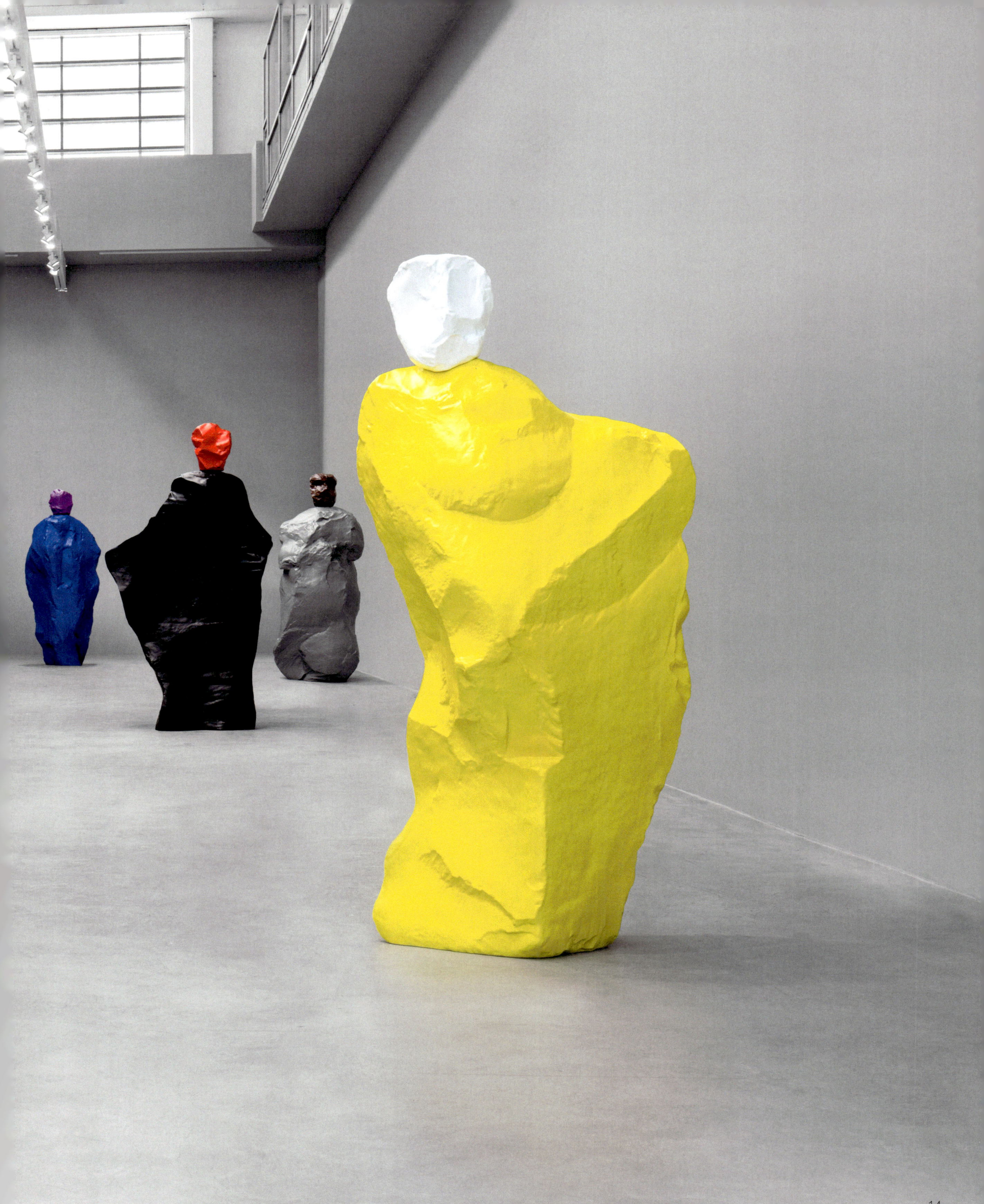

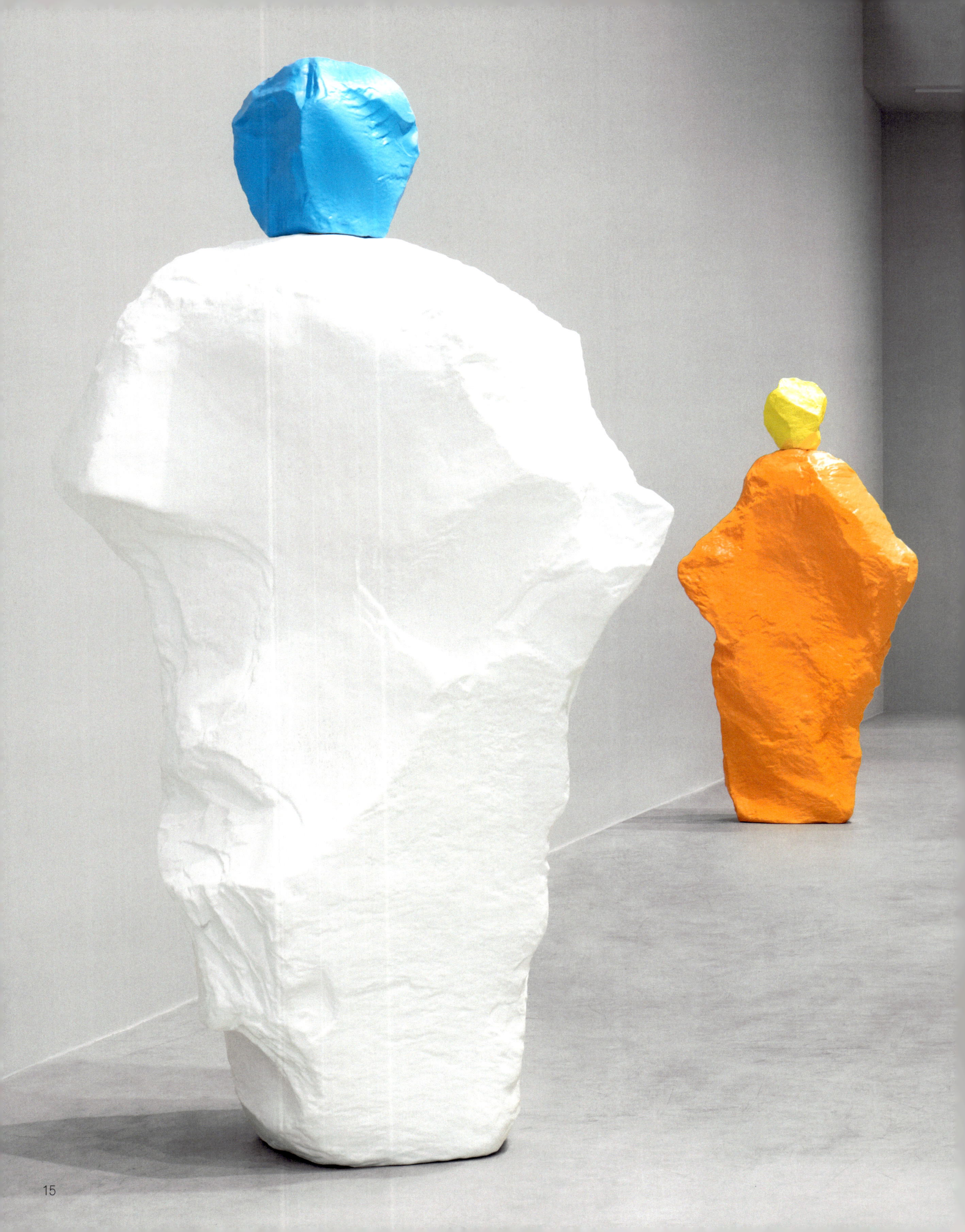

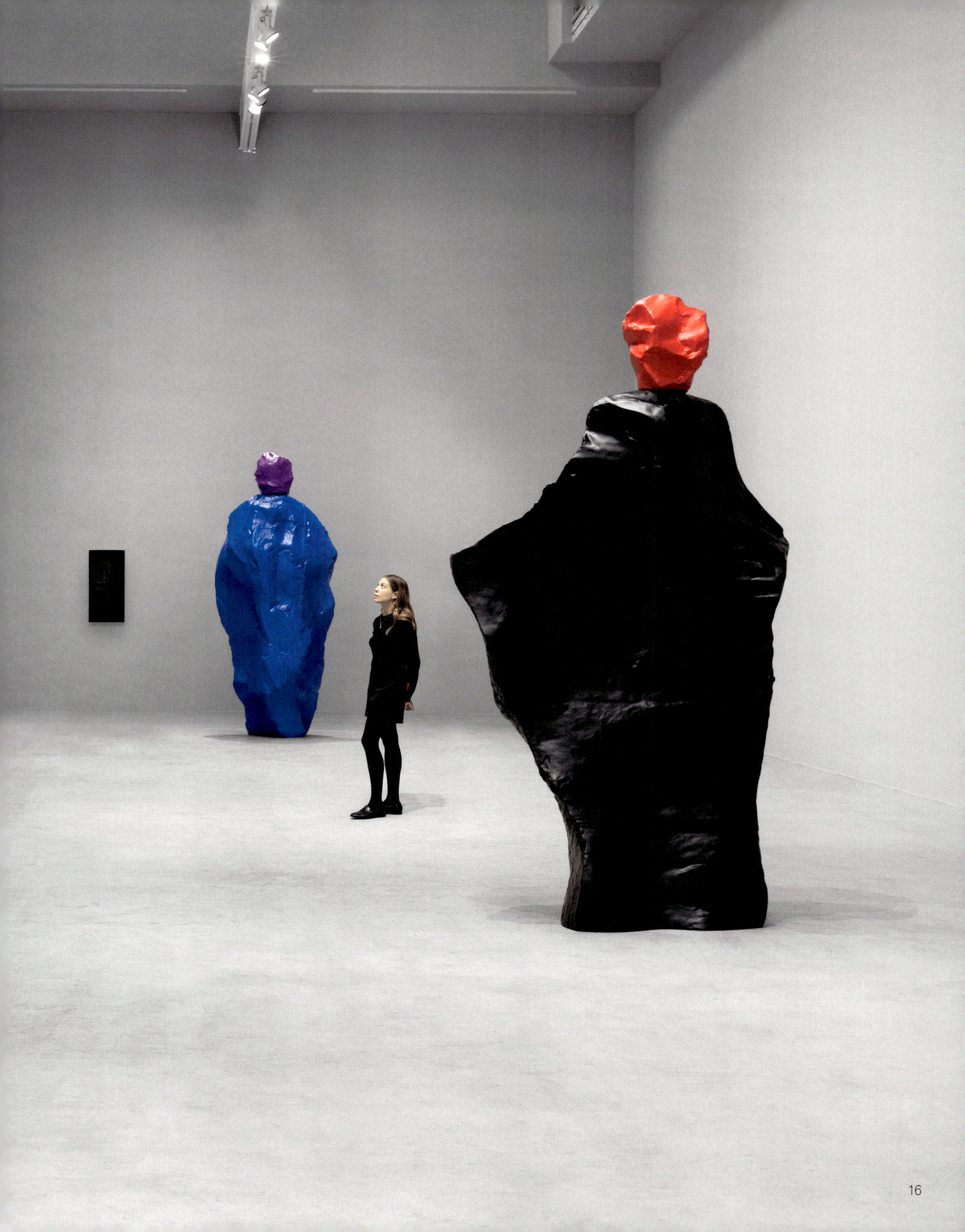

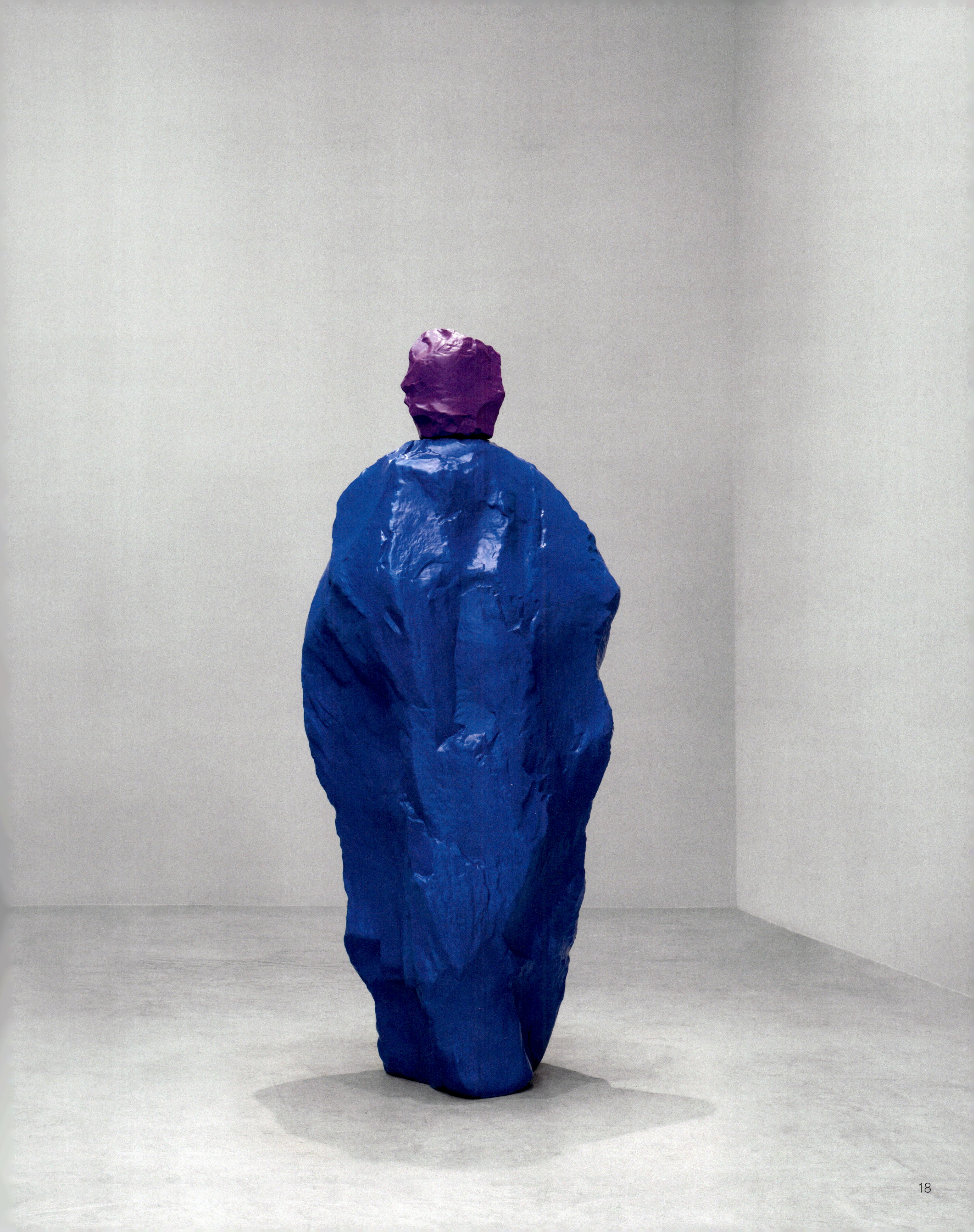

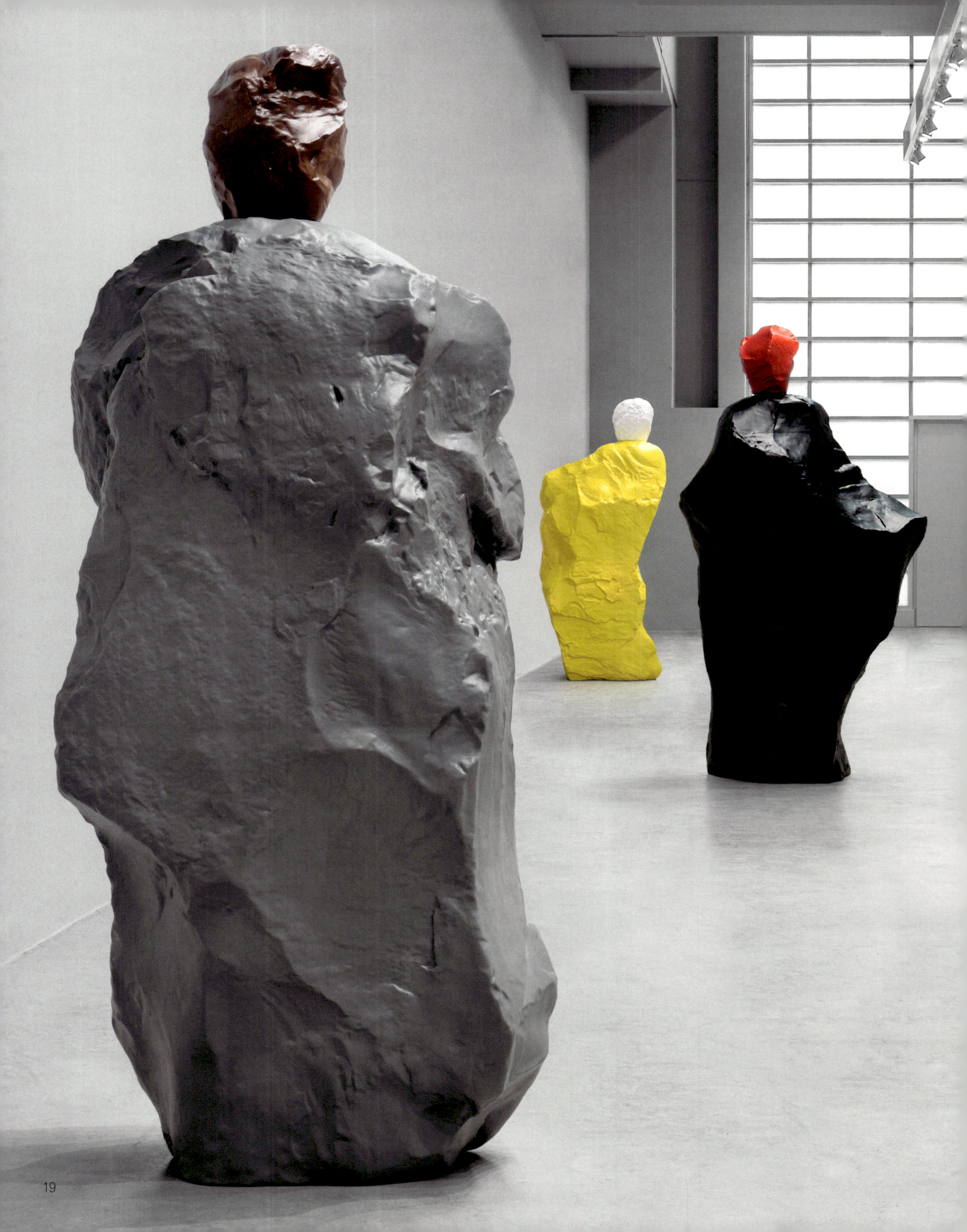

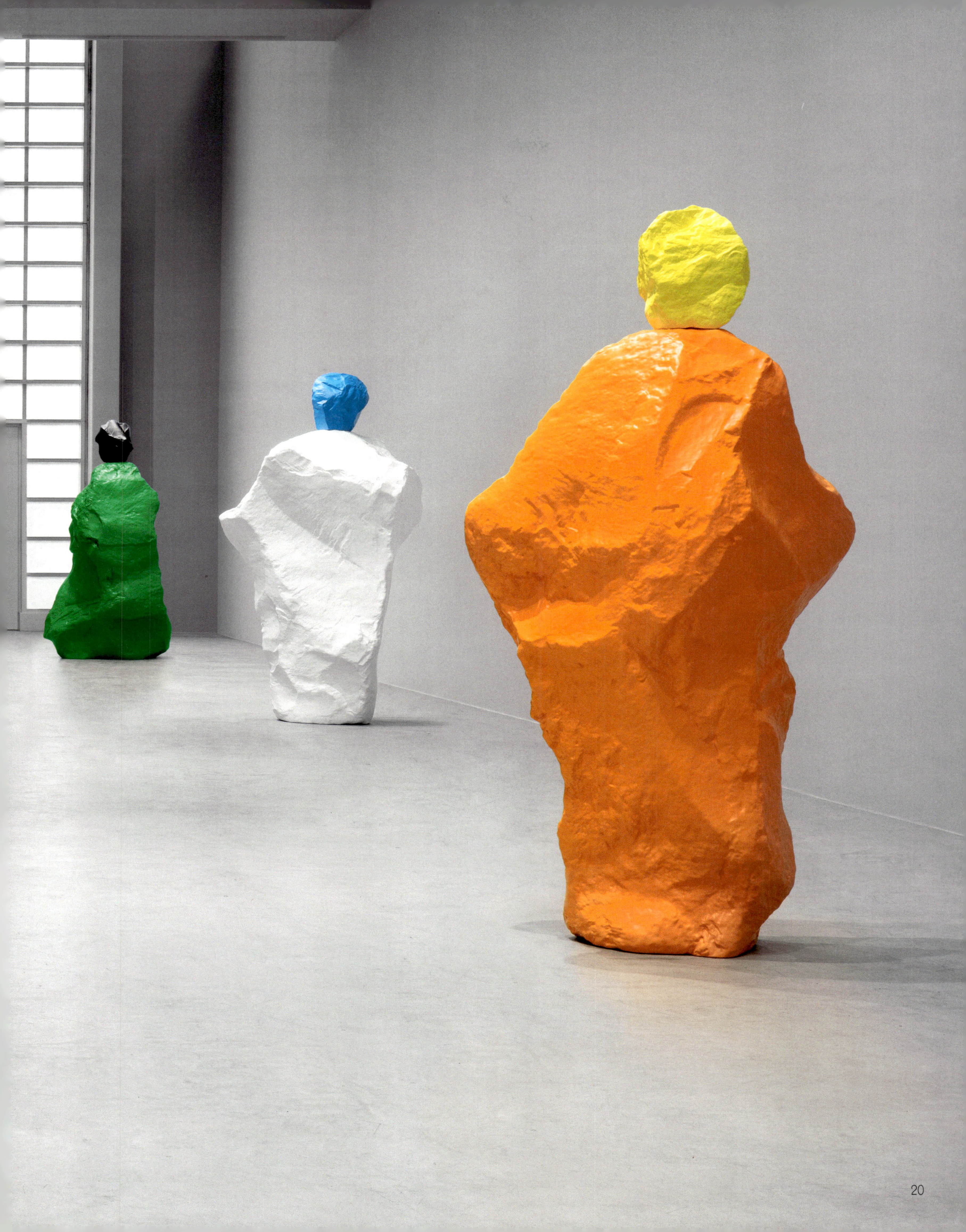

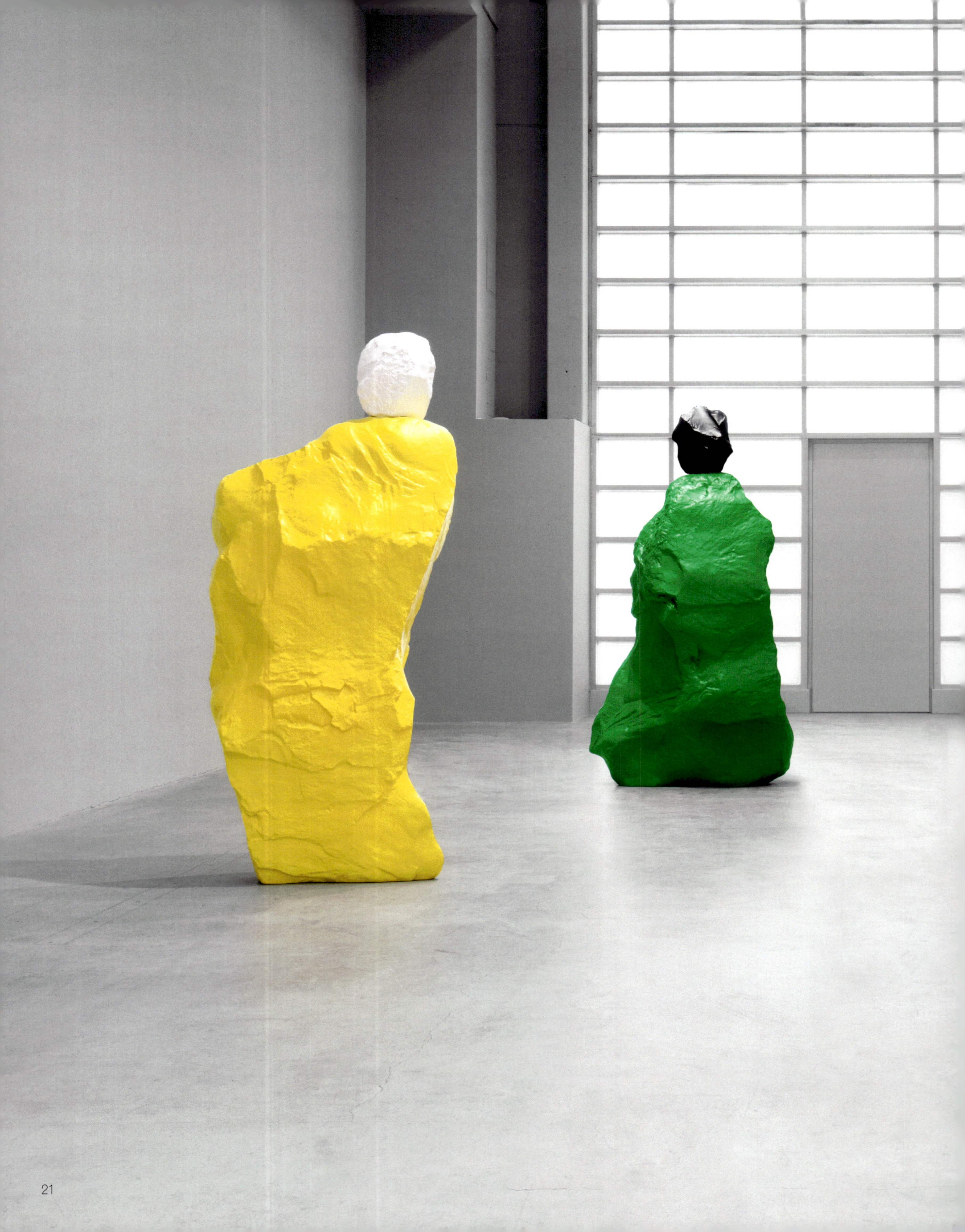

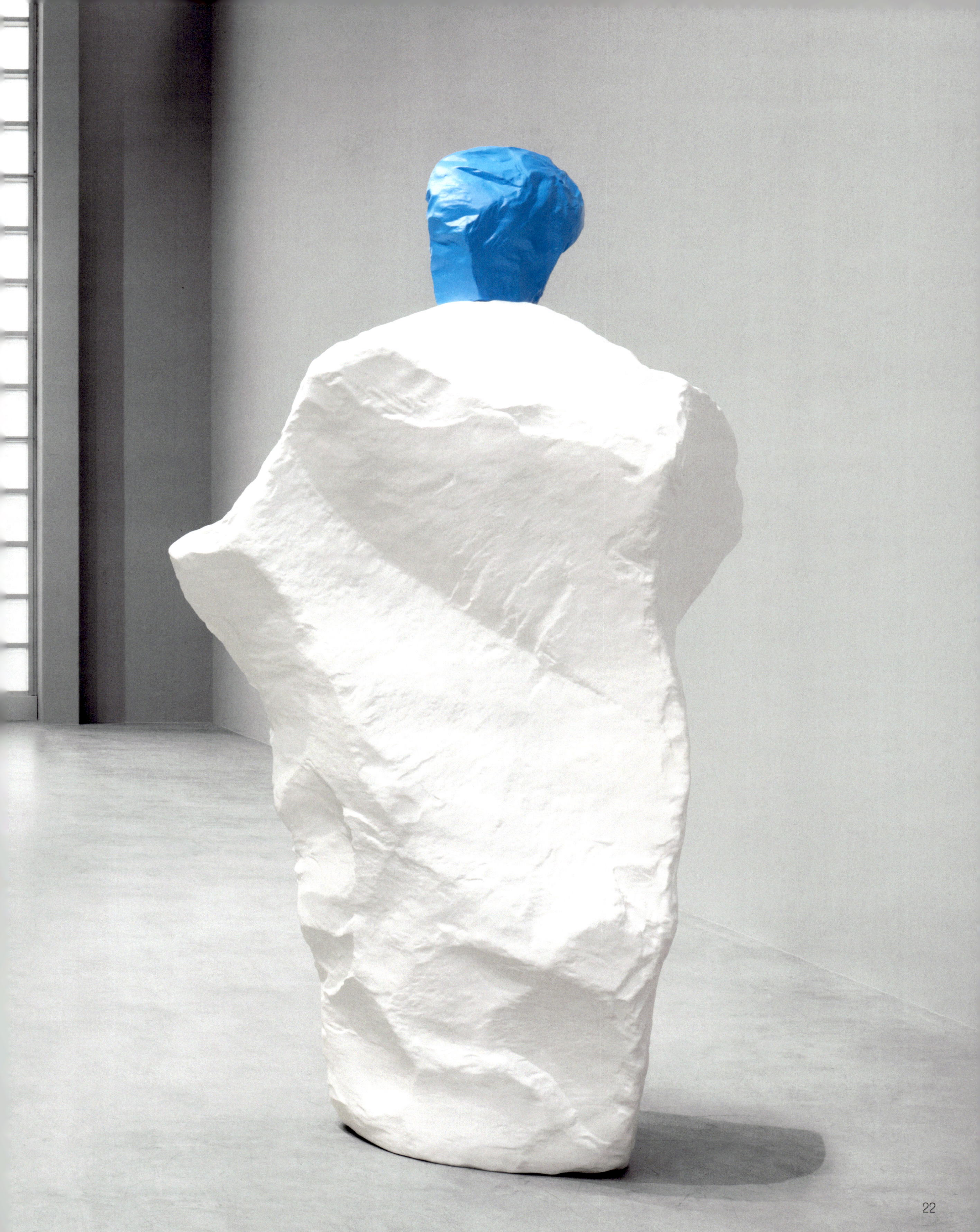

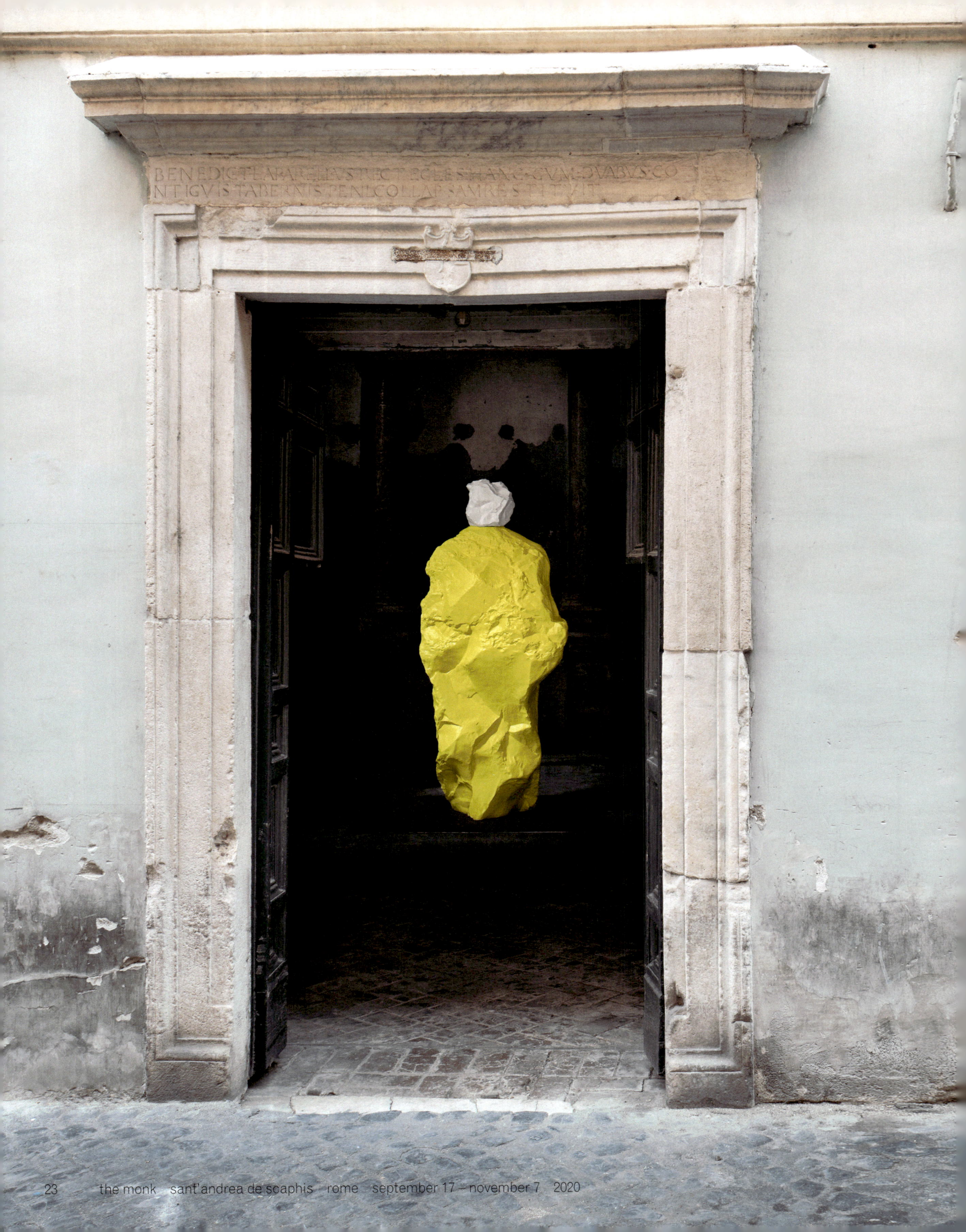

 the monk sant'andrea de scaphis rome september 17 – november 7 2020

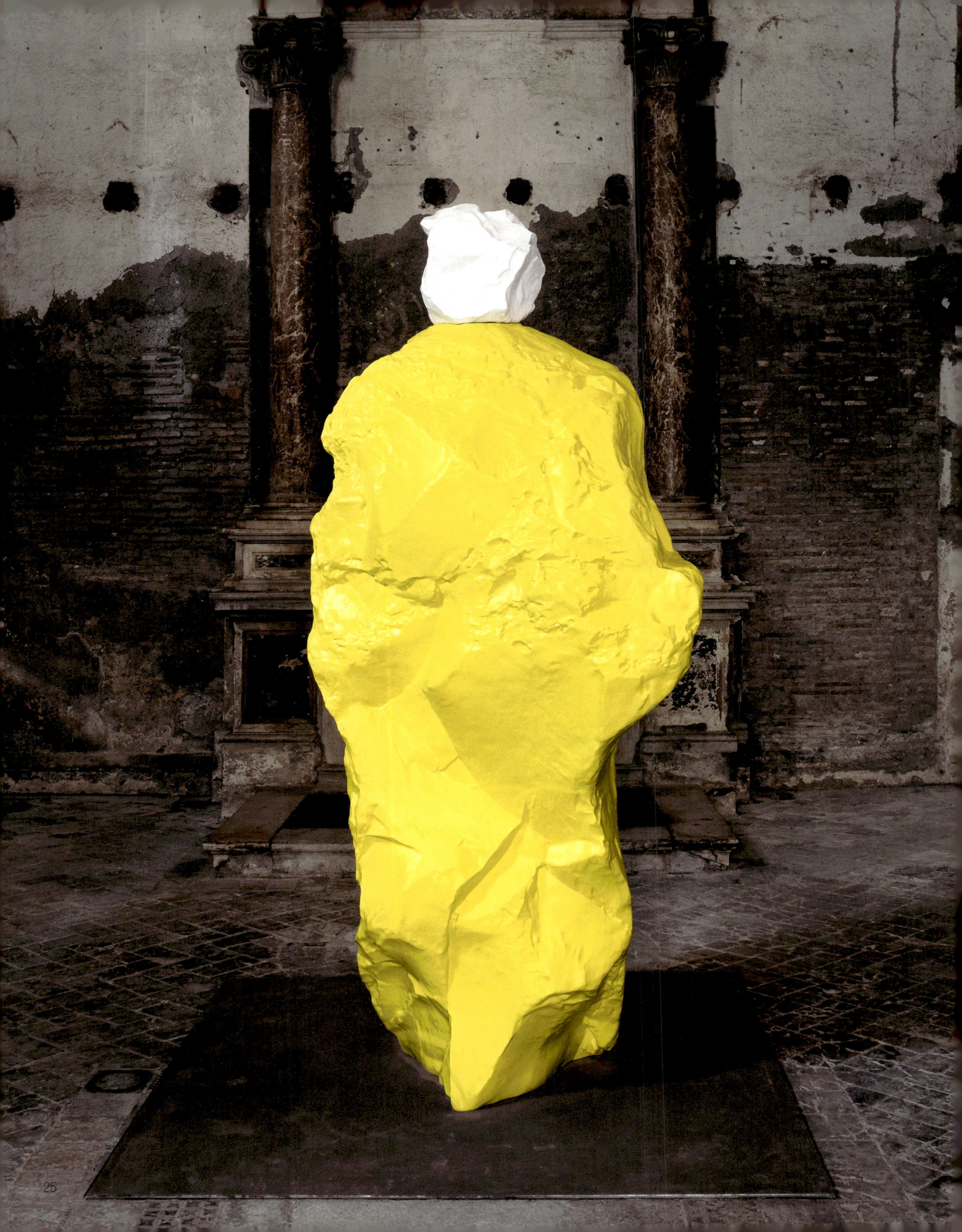

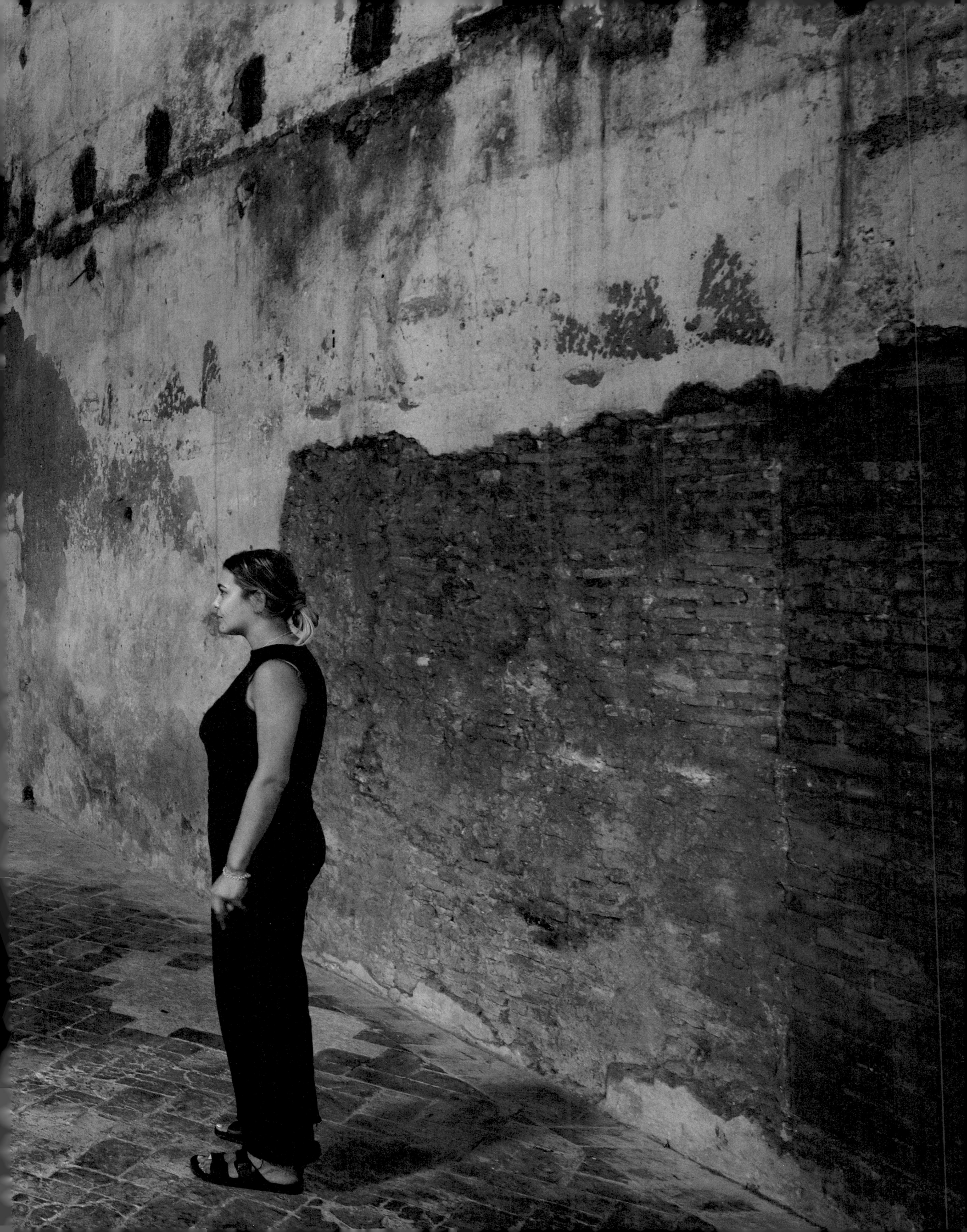

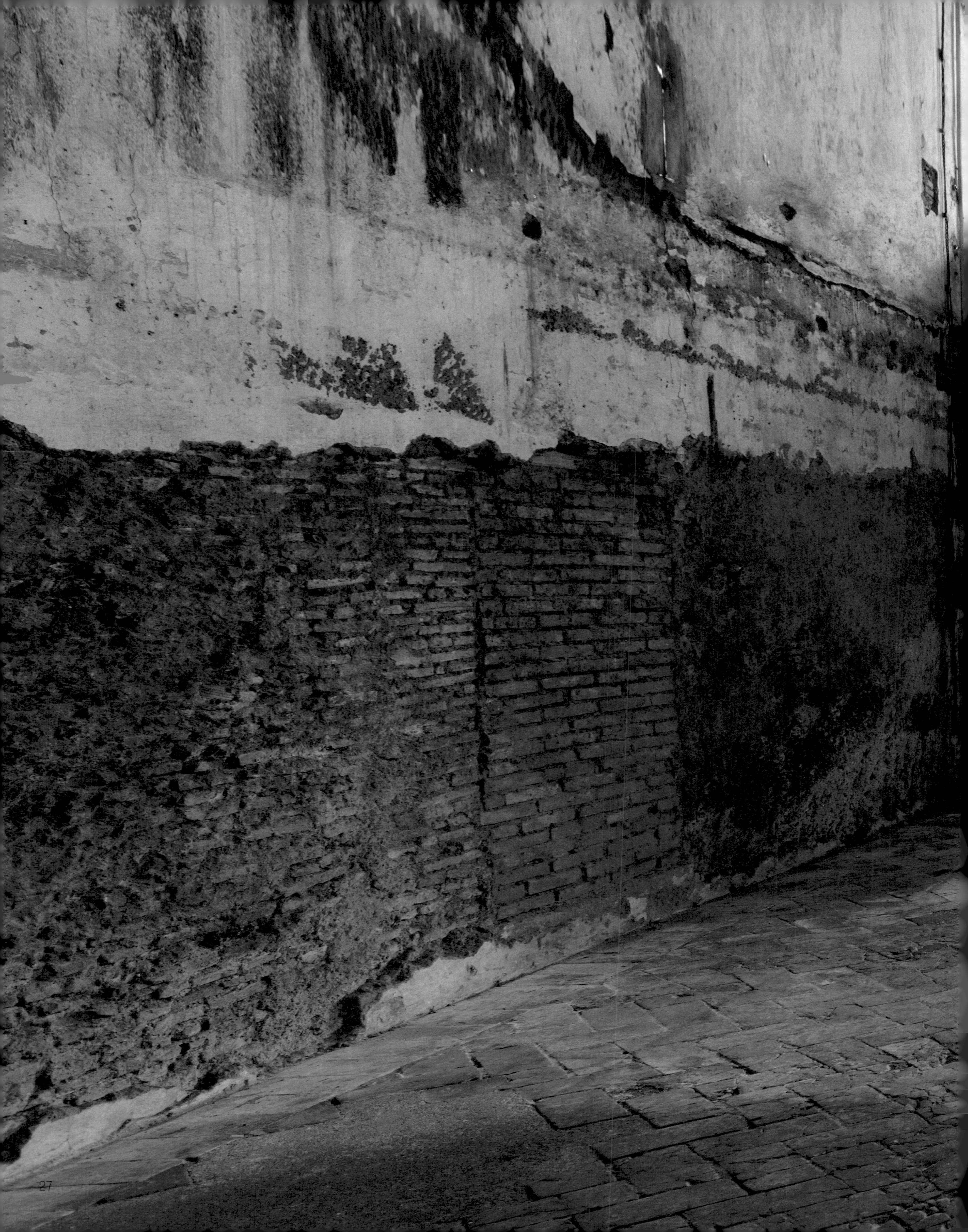

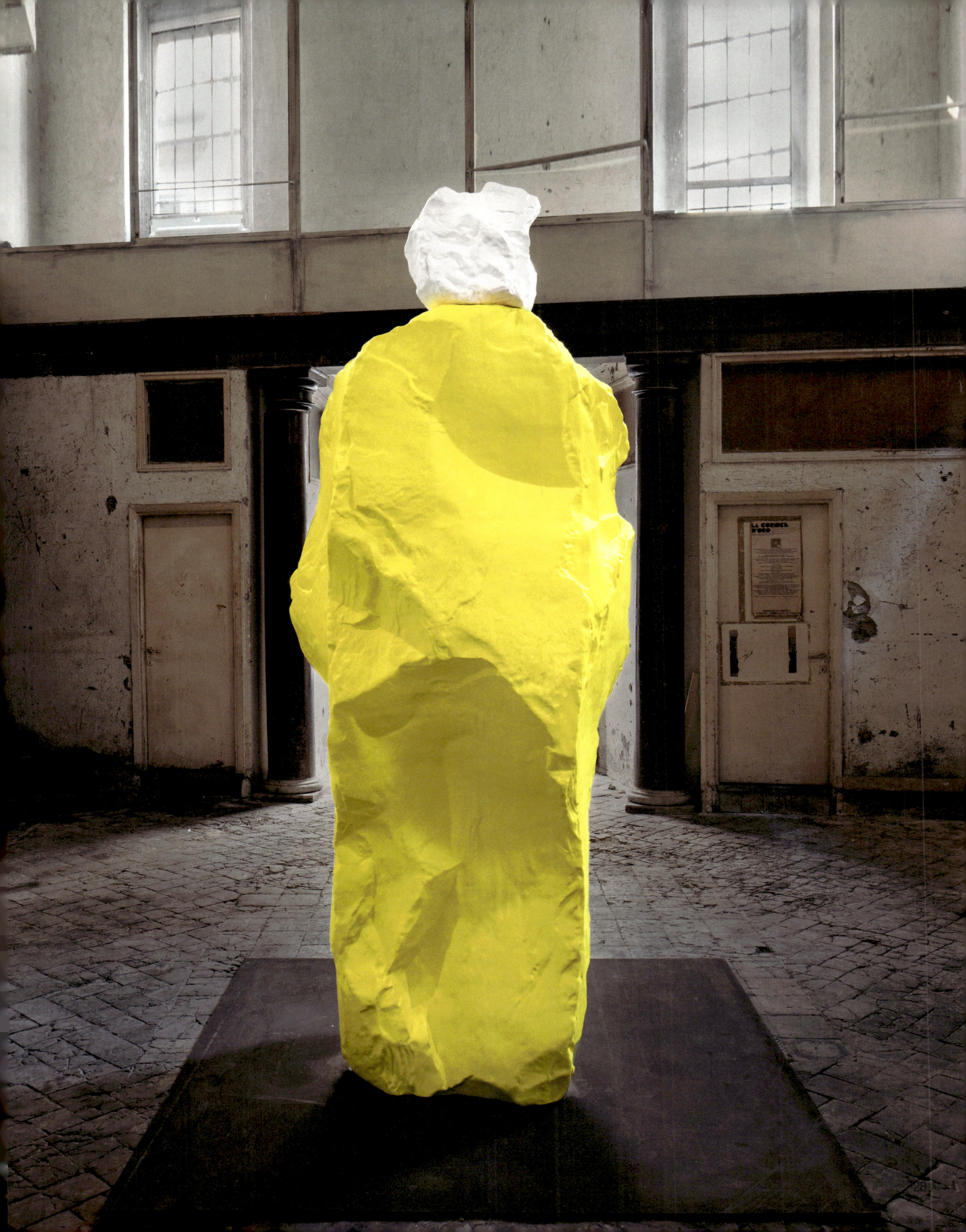
LA CORNICE D'ORO

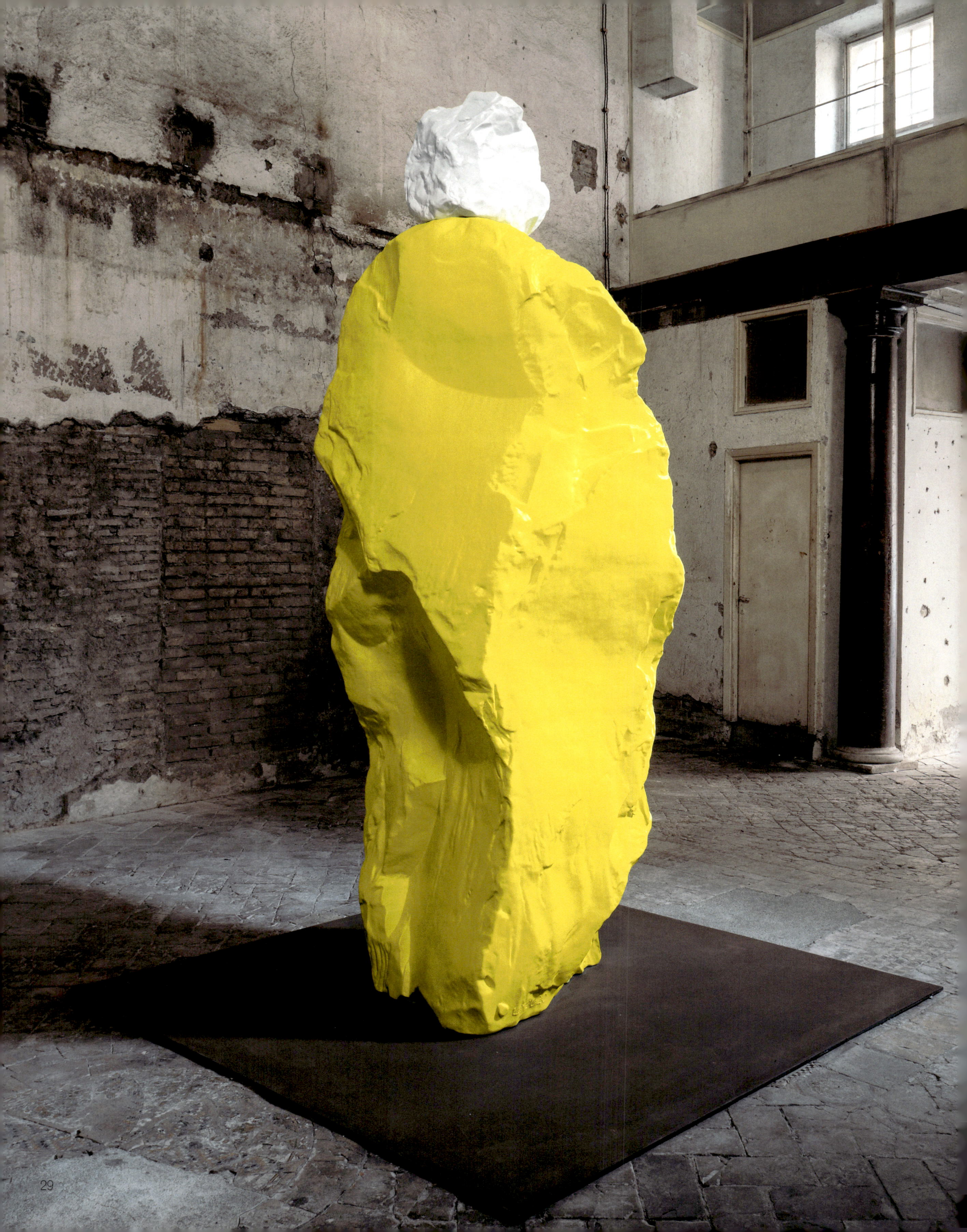

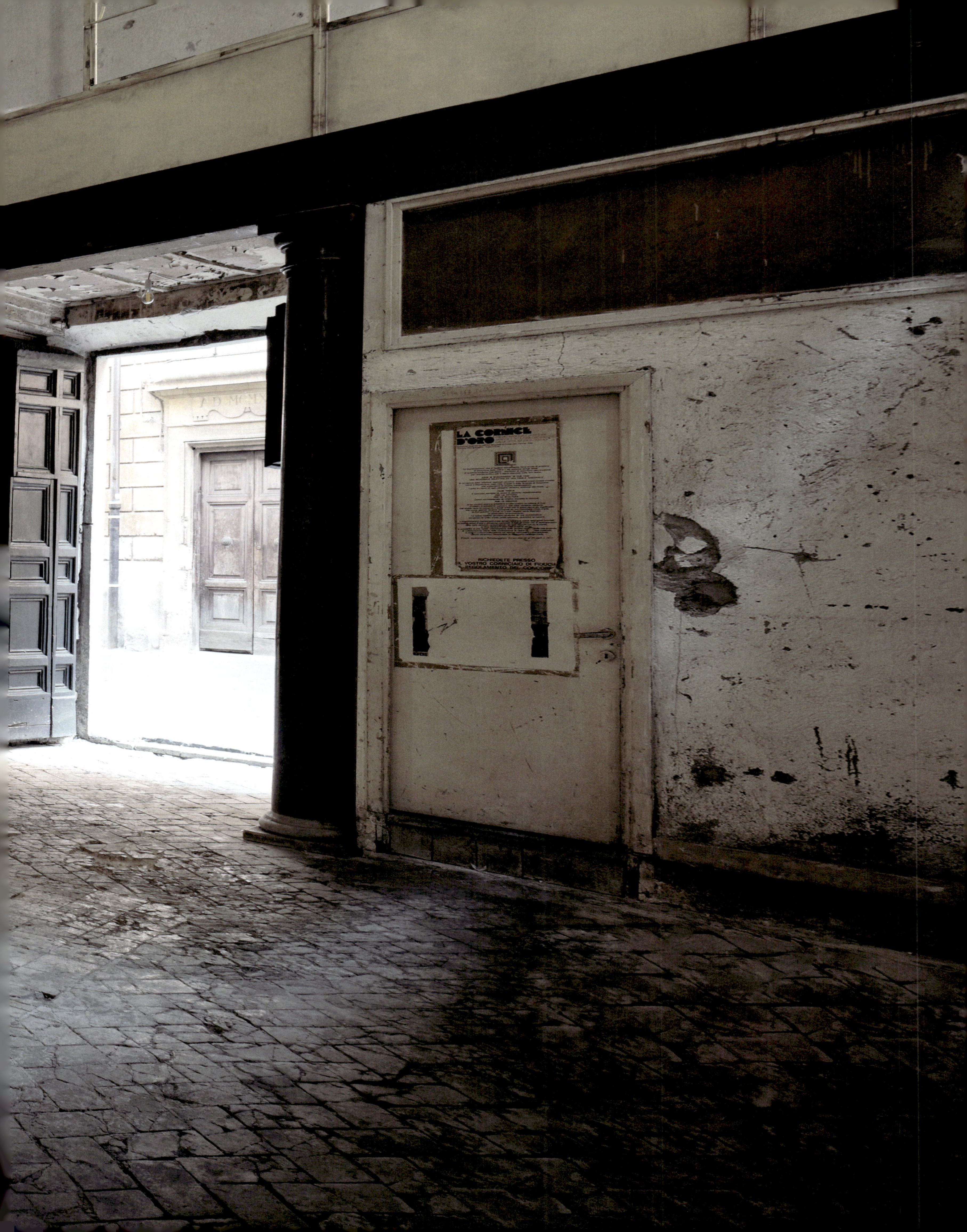
LA CORNICE D'ORO
RICHIEDETE PRESSO
IL VOSTRO CORNICIAIO DI FIDUCI
REGOLAMENTO DEL CONCOR

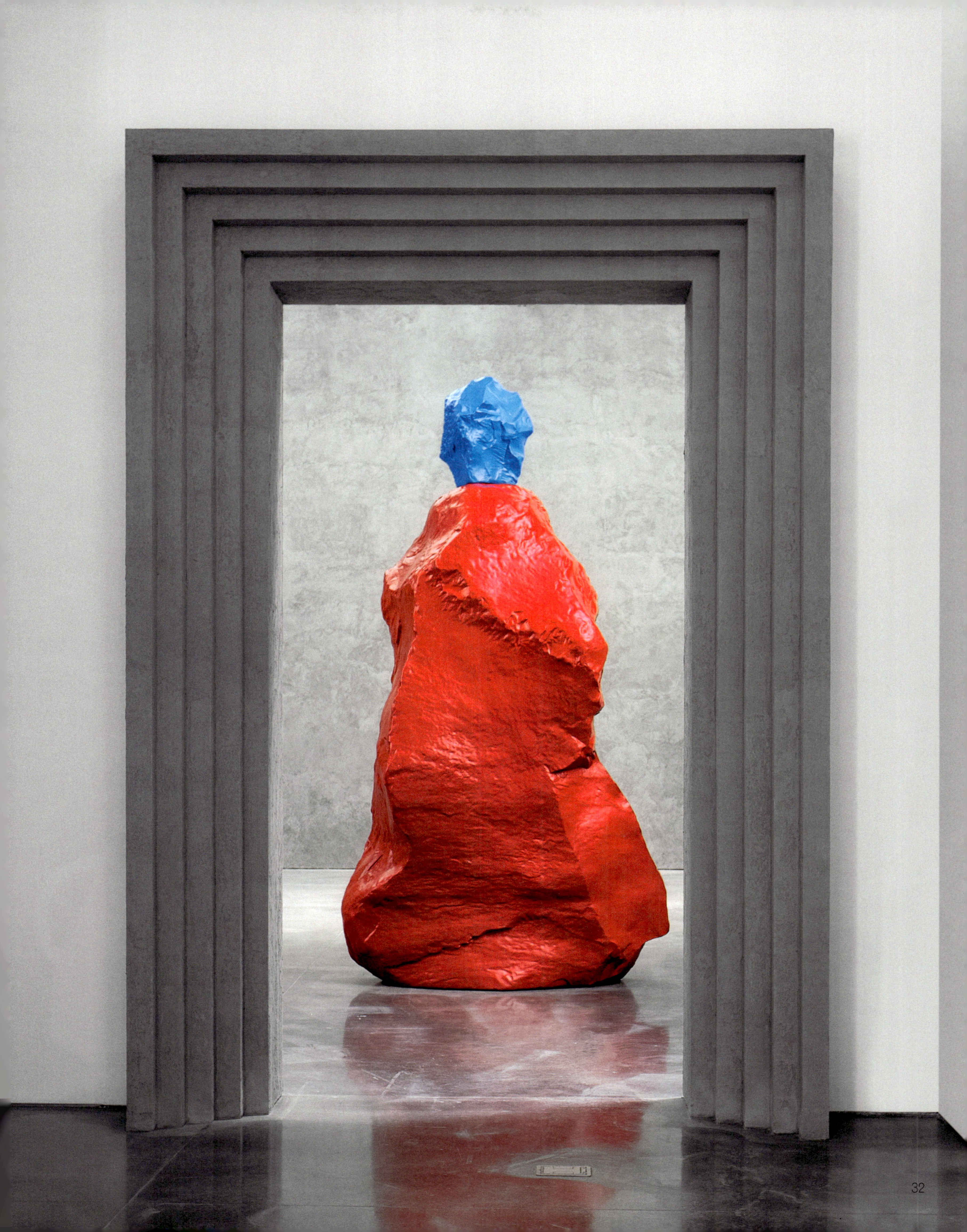

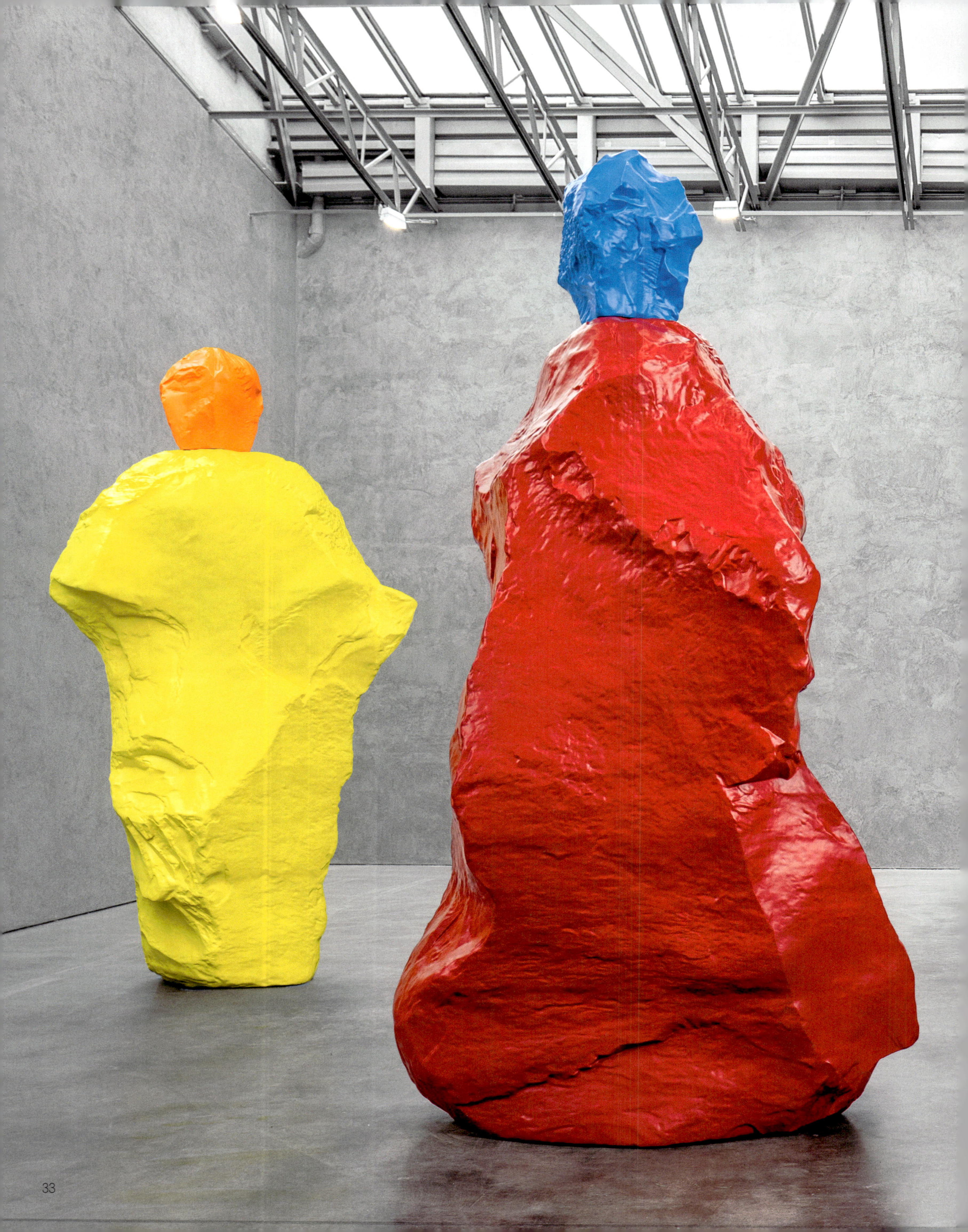

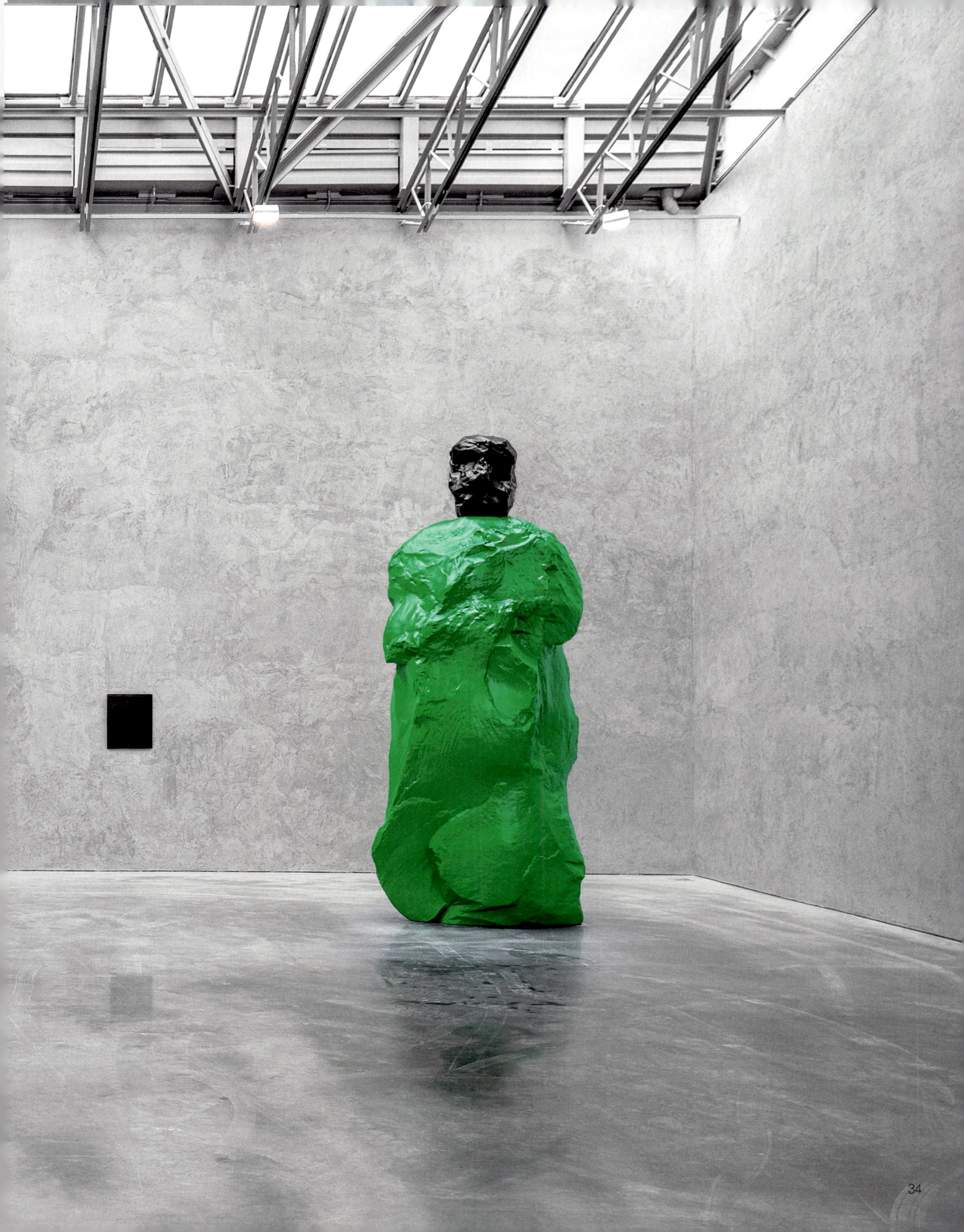

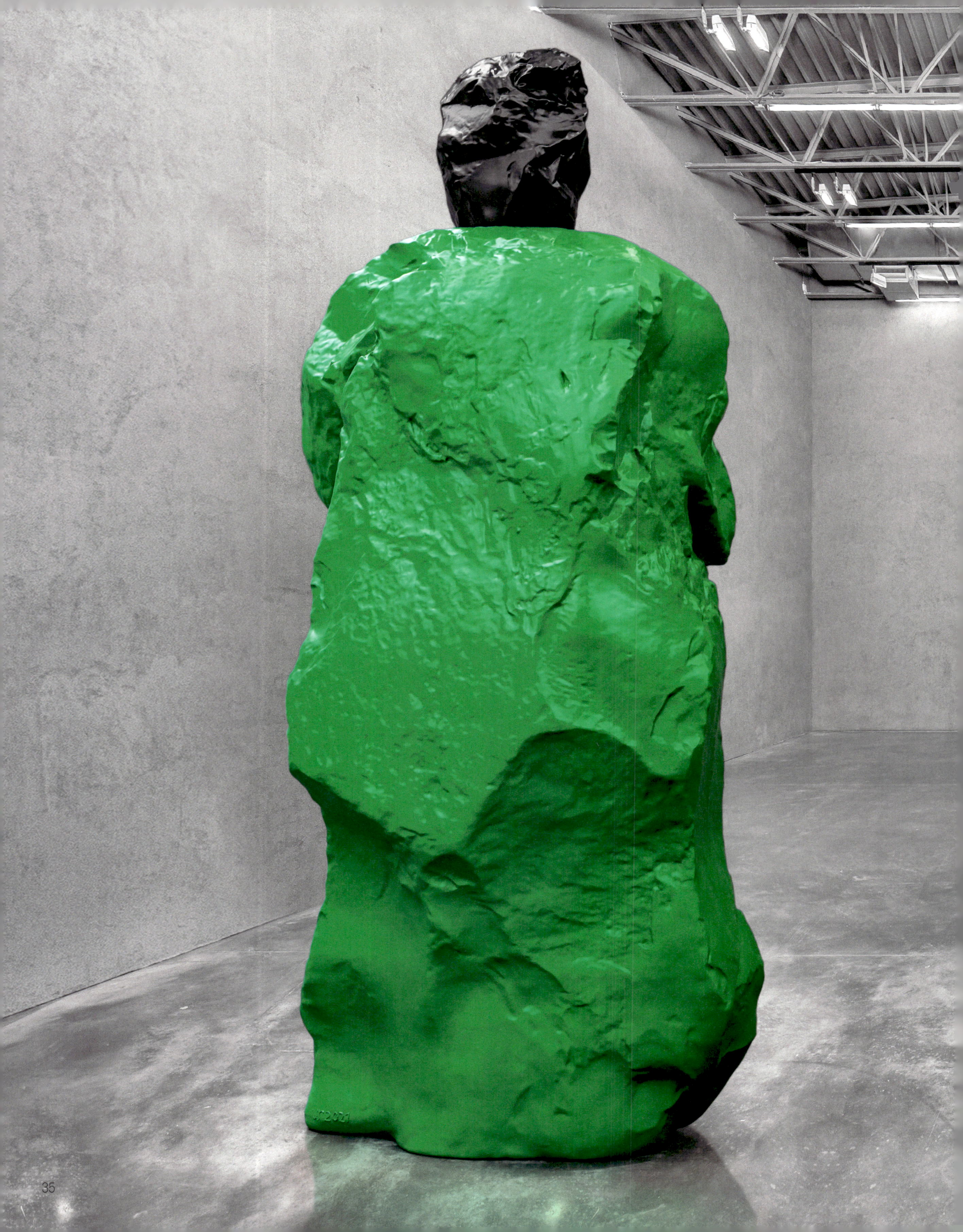

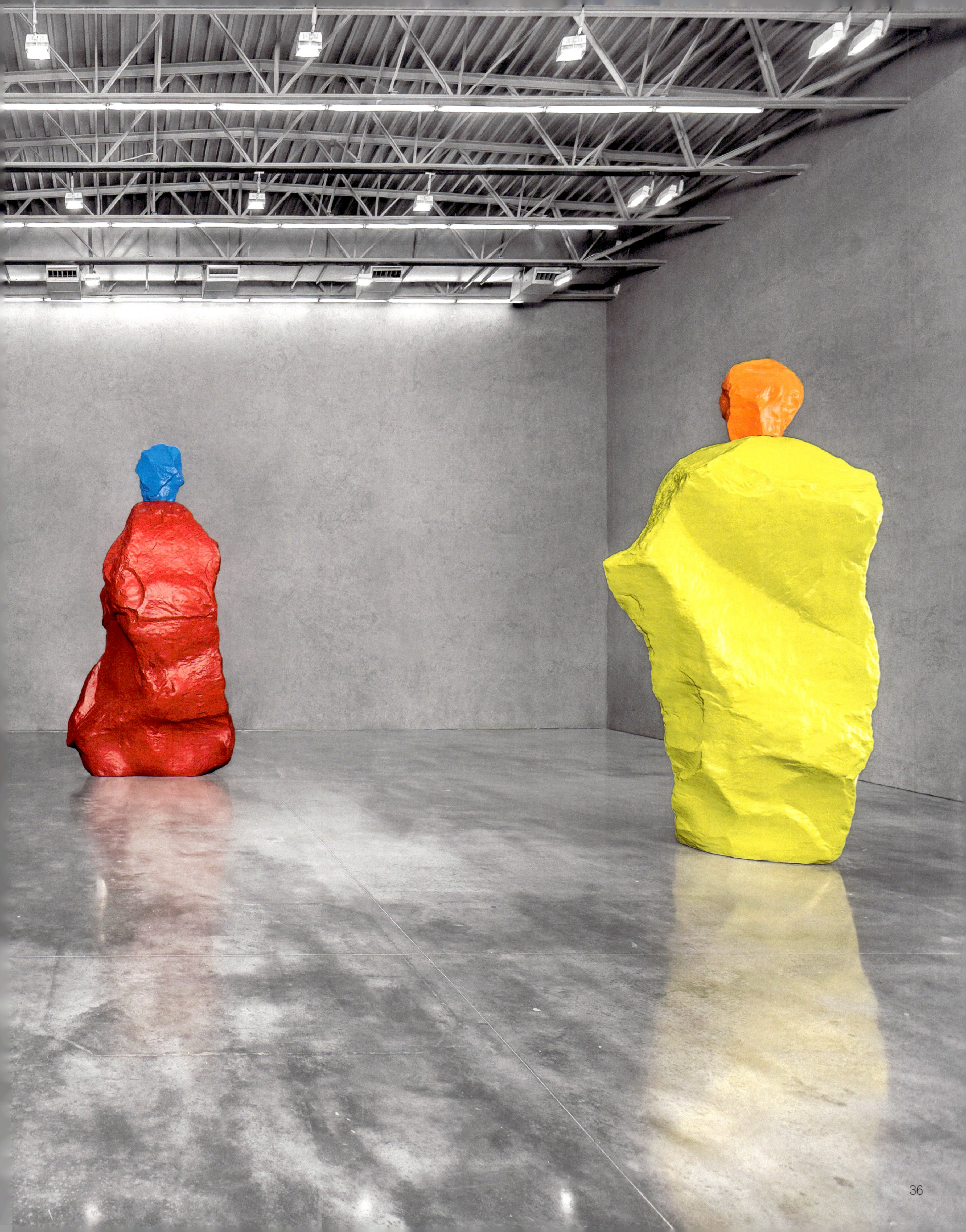

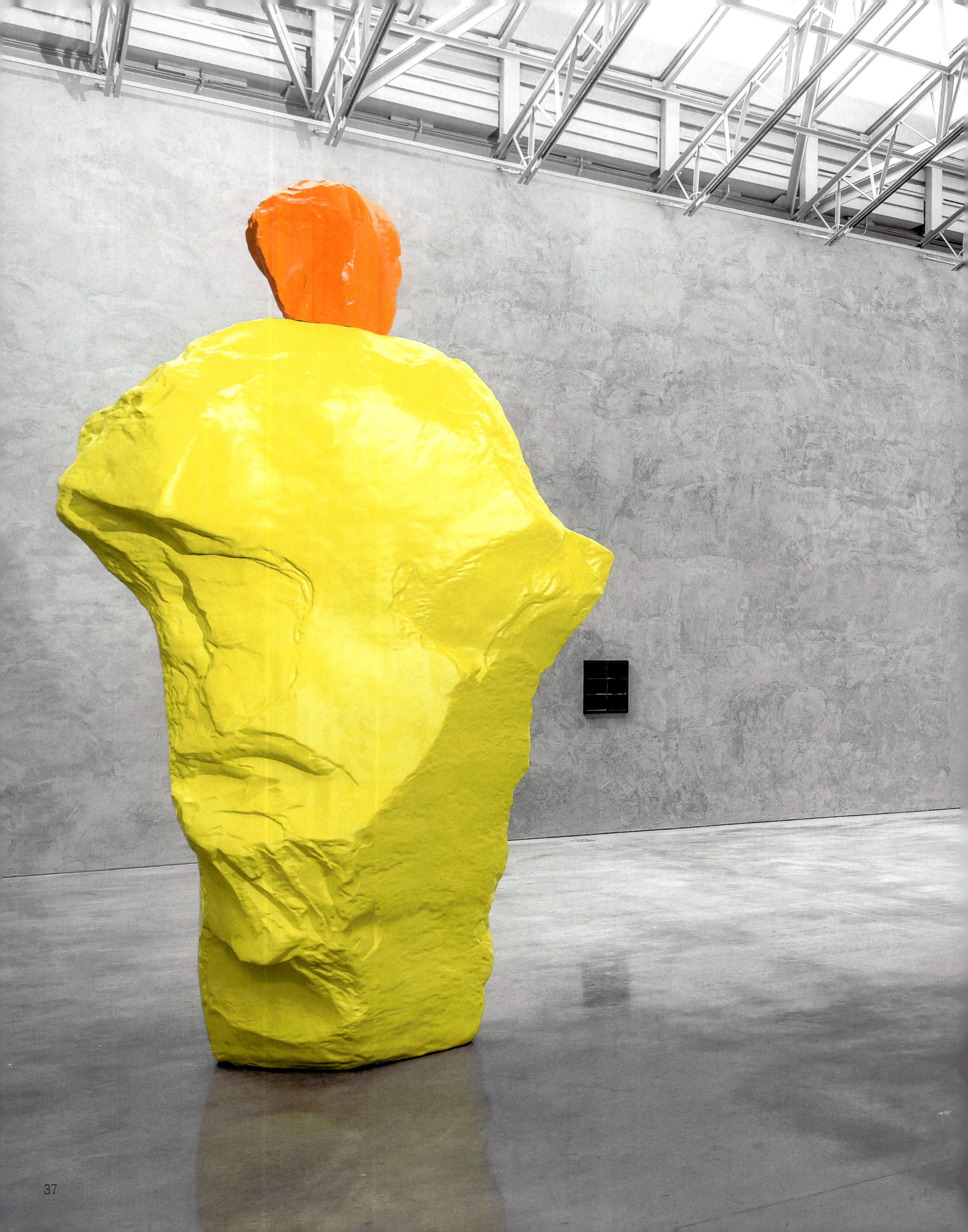

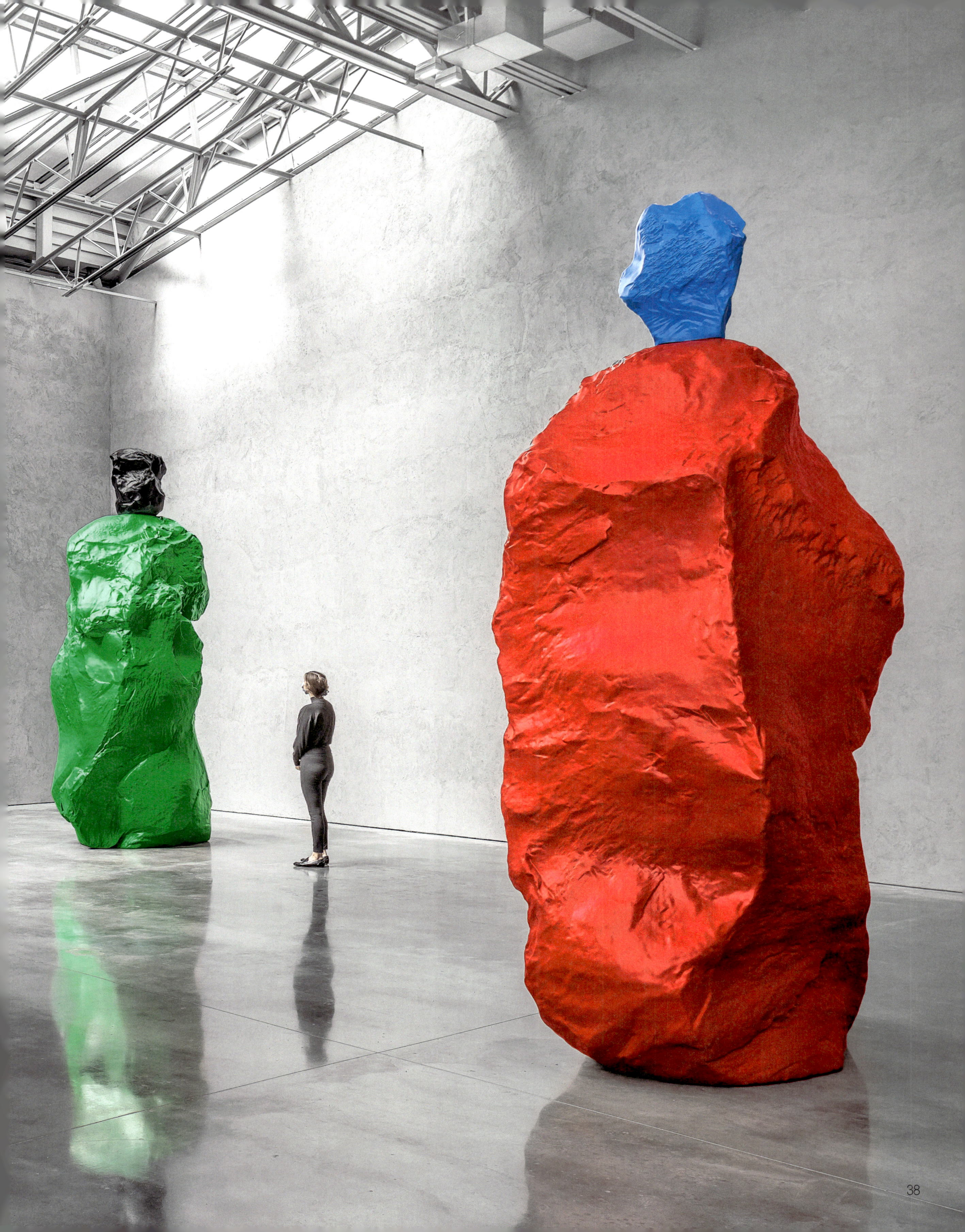

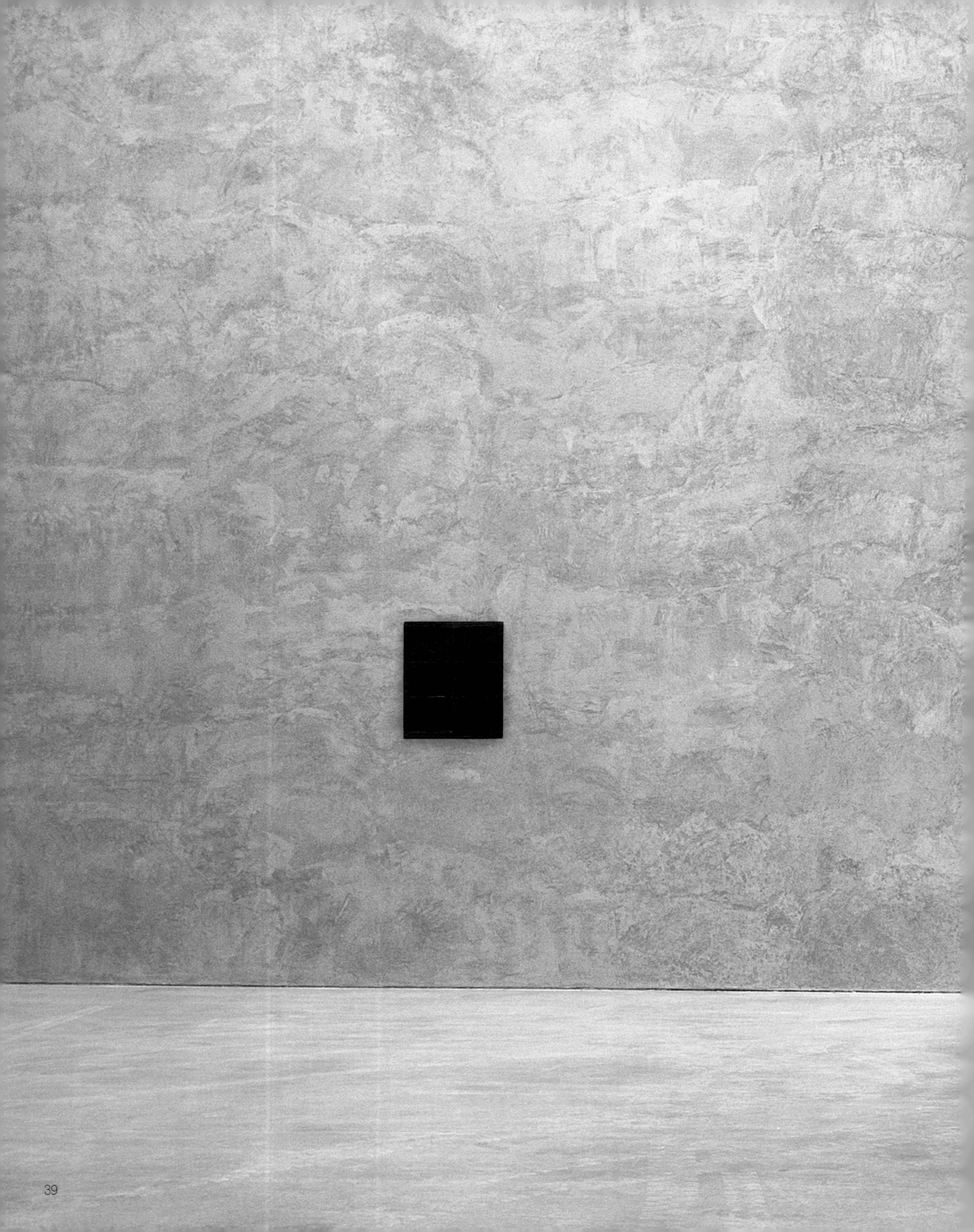

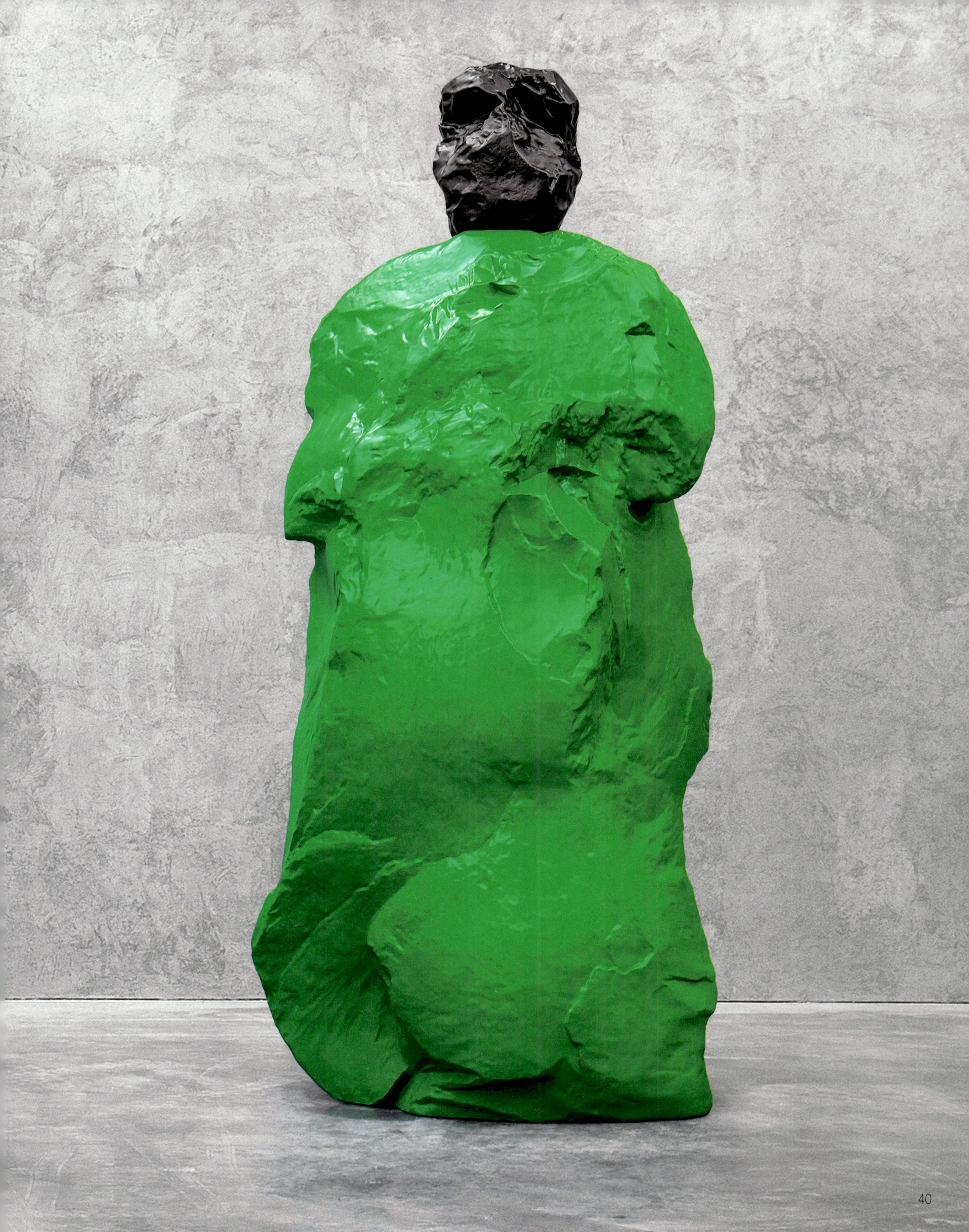

erik verhagen

transfigured matter

The recent sculptures nuns + monks by Ugo Rondinone take their rightful place in the continuity of a narrative introduced by the artist thirty-two years ago. A narrative composed of chapters that would never cease to interact with one another throughout a trajectory made up of intertextual questions, back-and-forths, survivals, displacements and reinventions of shapes and attitudes, or of interrogations that are constantly being renegotiated. This narrative originated in 1988 with the death of Manfred Kirchner, then Ugo Rondinone's partner, from an AIDS-related illness. "In the midst of the AIDS crisis, I turned away from my grief and found a spiritual guard rail in nature, a place for comfort, regeneration and inspiration. In nature, you enter a space where the sacred and the profane, the mystical and the secular vibrate against one another." The resulting works, landscapes with Romantic overtones painted in ink on paper, were first shown at the Kunstmuseum in Lucerne, then in several other exhibitions, including one at the Walcheturm gallery in Zürich, always with the same constraint: hung in confined spaces, their windows nailed shut with wooden boards, "cut off from the world", turned inward. From that point on, the opening up onto nature specific to the landscape found itself counterbalanced by a feeling of enclosure conducive to introspection. And a spiritual turning inward that would find itself perpetuated in the artist's self-portrait (Heyday), inspired by Joris-Karl Huysmans and his fictional character, the reclusive Jean des Esseintes, and shown in the framework of his exhibition cry me a river, also in Zürich, in 1995. Returned to its initial function, the window of the Walcheturm gallery was once again visible. In front of it was now a brown-painted frame and double pane, which opened like an arched backdrop through which one could see the self-portrait of the artist, portrayed as a passive figure, from the outside. The relationship between content and container, artwork and receptacle therefore responded to an inverted antagonistic principle. But *in fine* a precarious, equivalent equilibrium had been achieved, from which the spirituality expressed by the artist via the different chapters of the narrative in progress would then unfold.

The nuns + monks sculptures express in turn this dialectic from within and without. From opening up onto the world and from turning inward on oneself. From an introspective gaze combined with an exteriority receptive to nature's elements of which these sculptures bear the traces. *The imprint*. Rondinone's works have never stopped oscillating between extremes, entangling, suspending them. *Aufheben...* The sculptures of nuns + monks possess a natural beauty. An "archaic" beauty that evokes other sculptural ensembles by the artist: Human Nature on Rockefeller Plaza in 2013 and Seven Magic Mountains in the Nevada desert in 2016. They manifest visibility yet at the same time seem to avoid the gaze of those to whom they are shown. Their features are indistinct. And in this era of multiple gender identities, they are divested of sexual characteristics, even though their titles allow us to *differentiate* them. It would certainly be extremely difficult to distinguish the nuns from the monks based on their mere appearance. Wrapped and protected in their cloaks, they seem, like his 1995 self-portrait and the ensuing clowns and nudes, *absorbed*, in the same way that Diderot characterized the figures depicted in certain paintings by Chardin. Absorbed in what? In whom? In the spectators wandering around them? In the architectural space that serves as the backdrop for their paradoxically motionless choreography? Unless, as is extremely likely, the space in question is mental. *Meditative.* Transcending the matter that still seems to determine their heft. Or, more than *transcended*, one could say the matter in nuns + monks is *transfigured*, revealing a *radiance* reinforced by the chromatic contrasts, the harmony generated by the juxtaposition of different body parts—the head and the cloak—and by the sculptures, perfectly integrated from one to the next, the abovementioned radiance evoking medieval statuary serving the same religious and spiritual purpose to which the artist is deeply committed. It should be explained that the creation of these works was nourished by Rondinone's assiduous frequentation of the medieval sculpture department at the Metropolitan Museum in New York, and in addition by a powerful confrontation with Giacomo Manzù's cardinals, whose own particular modernity, permeated by a classicism that defies time and categorization, inevitably corresponded to his interest.

Between matter and its negation, these sculptures invest a polarized field. *Amphibological*. Made in bronze, they were conceived from limestone models, scans of which were "three-dimensionalized" with digital tools. In response to the friable limestone, the solidity of the bronze. In response to the stone's natural, ancient origins, the *here and now* contemporaneity of the polychrome castings. Of course, we must, as is often the case in Rondinone's work, seek the response, ineluctably unstable, inherent in his propositions in the interpenetration of the extremes and intervals they bring about. In a game of equivalences. Opening up onto the world, to nature, and turning inward on oneself. In matter that is as embodied as it is disembodied. And given its elevated spiritual coefficient, so remarkable these days and, in a manner of speaking, absent from contemporary art, in an *anagogical* principle that re-transcribes and accompanies the process of transfiguration underlying this group of sculptures.

translated from french by laurie hurvitz

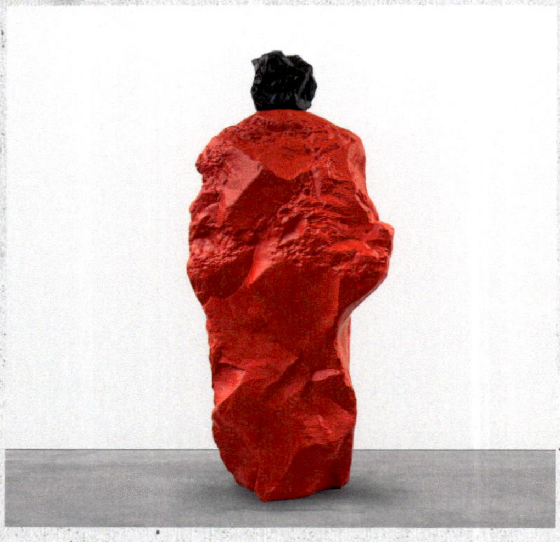

black red nun, 2020
painted bronze
295 x 121 x 115 cm
unique

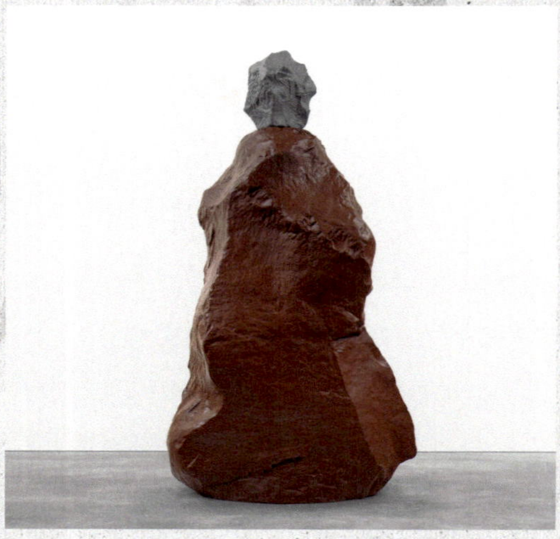

gray brown nun, 2020
painted bronze
294 x 157 x 100 cm
unique

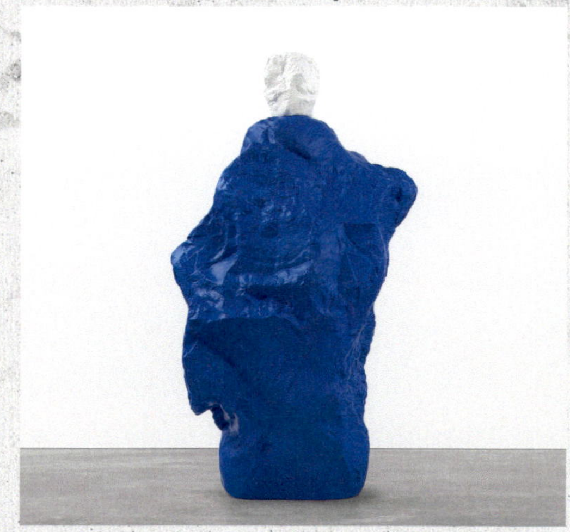

white blue monk, 2020
painted bronze
297 x 157 x 122 cm
unique

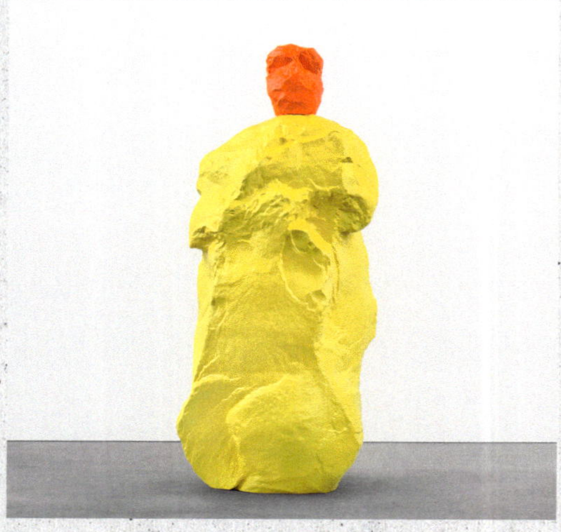

orange yellow monk, 2020
painted bronze
294 x 131 x 102 cm
unique

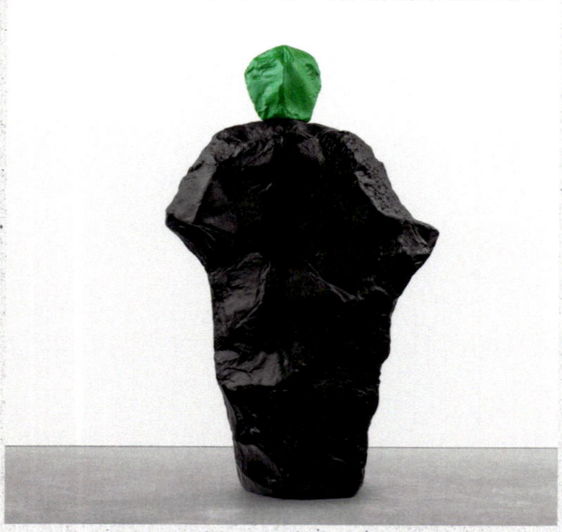

green black monk, 2020
painted bronze
295 x 171 x 97 cm
unique

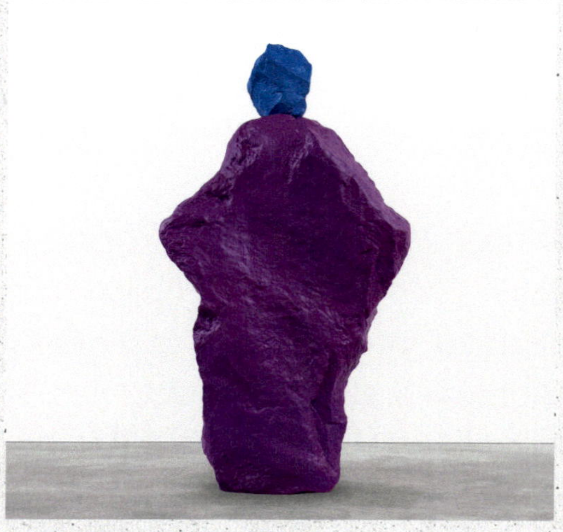

blue violet nun, 2020
painted bronze
293 x 157 x 80 cm
unique

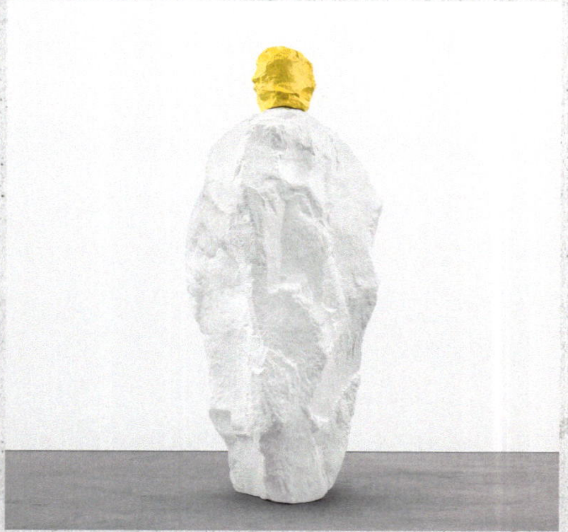

yellow white monk, 2020
painted bronze
295 x 125 x 93 cm
unique

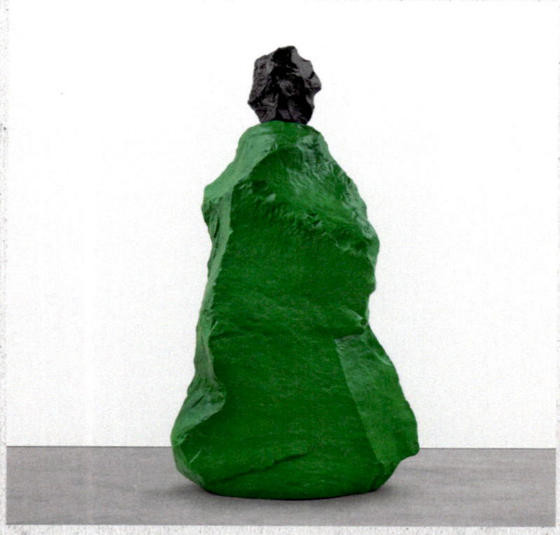

black green monk, 2020
painted bronze
294 x 157 x 100
unique

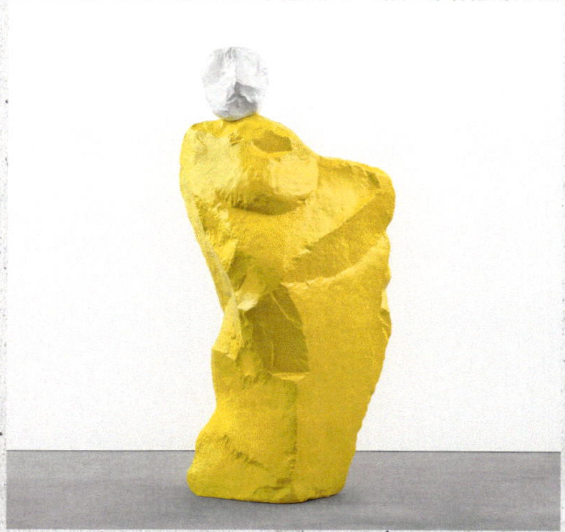

white yellow nun, 2020
painted bronze
292 x 135 x 90 cm
unique

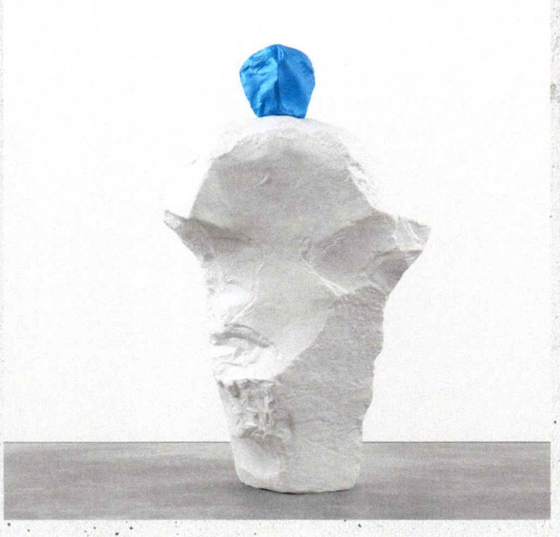

blue white monk, 2020
painted bronze
295 x 170 x 97 cm
unique

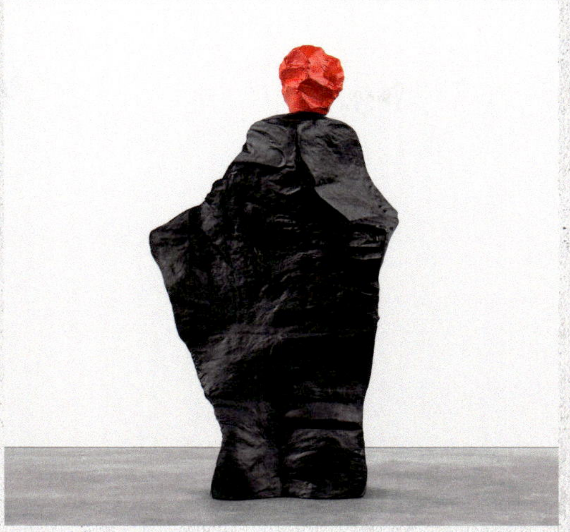

red black monk, 2020
painted bronze
292 x 158 x 105 cm
unique

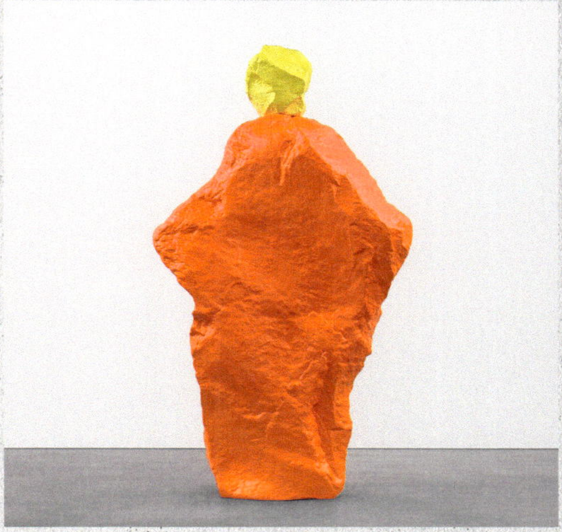

yellow orange monk, 2020
painted bronze
293 x 157 x 80 cm
unique

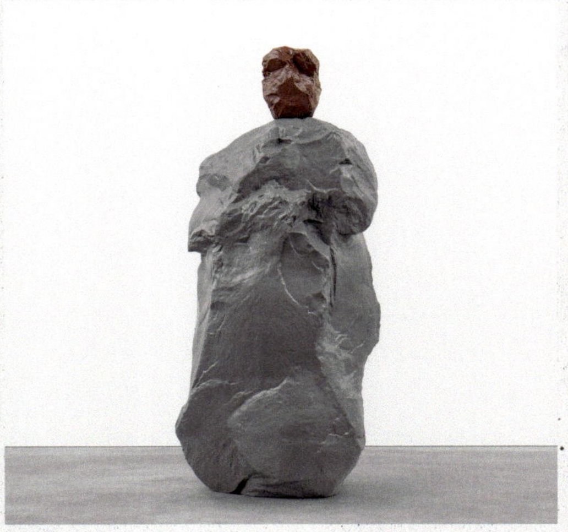

brown gray nun, 2020
painted bronze
294 x 131 x 102 cm
unique

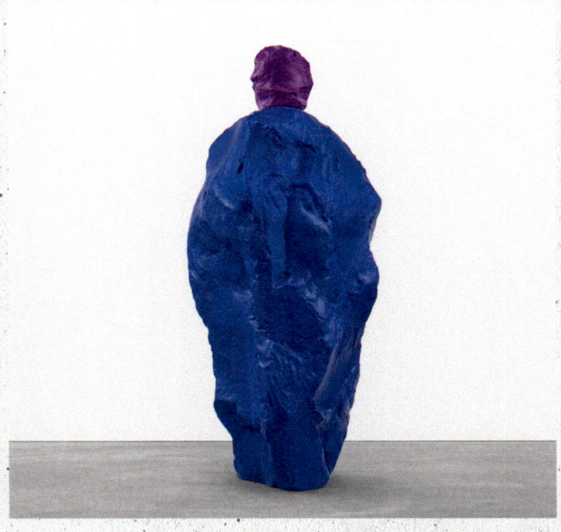

violet blue nun, 2020
painted bronze
295 x 125 x 93 cm
unique

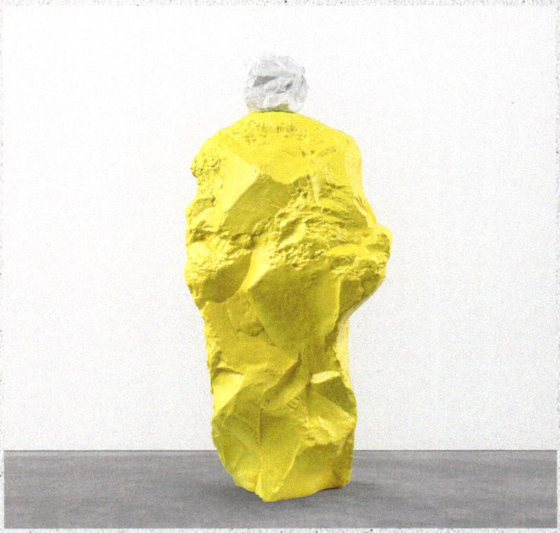

white yellow monk, 2020
painted bronze
295 x 121 x 114 cm
unique

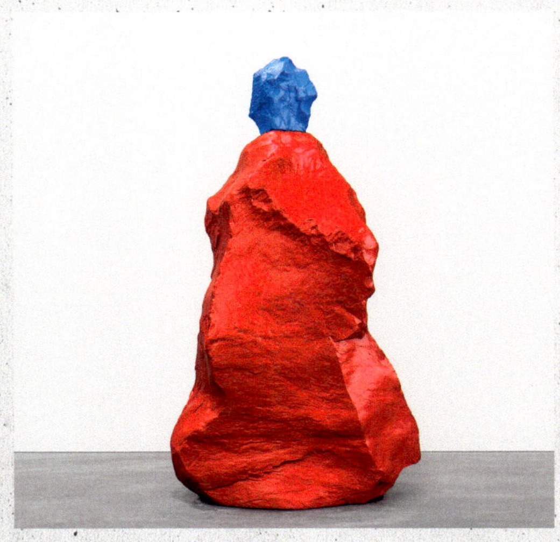

blue red nun, 2021
painted bronze
400 x 222 x 141 cm
unique

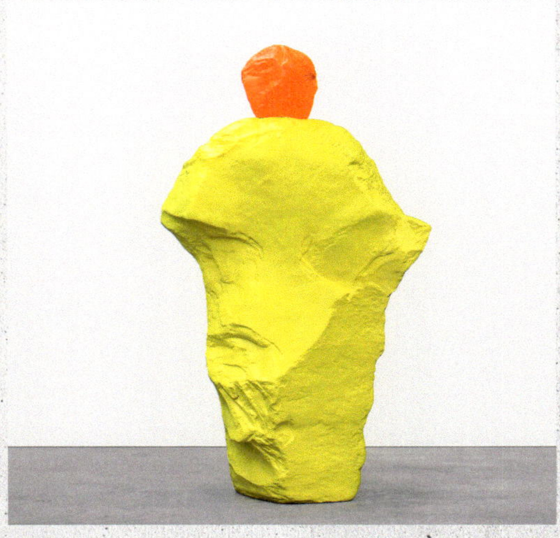

orange yellow nun, 2021
painted bronze
400 x 212 x 152 cm
unique

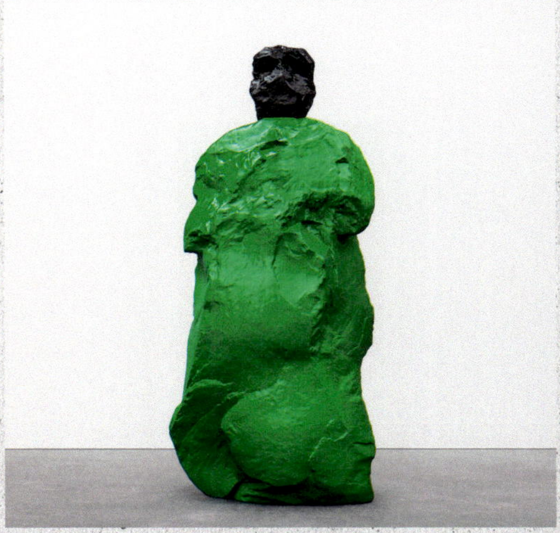

black green monk, 2021
painted bronze
400 x 177 x 146 cm
unique

drifting clouds 1820, 2016
cast aluminum
80 x 50 x 4 cm
ed 1 of 2 + 2 ap

fog in the elbe valley 1821, 2016
cast aluminum
73 x 30 x 14 cm
ed 1 of 2 + 2 ap

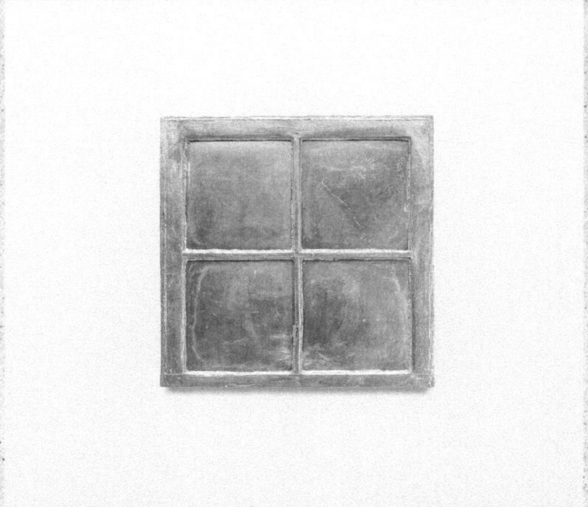

mountain landscape with rainbow 1810, 2016
cast aluminum
66 x 63 x 4 cm
ed 1 of 2 + 2 ap

man and woman contemplating the moon 1824, 2015
cast aluminum
90 x 40 x 3 cm
ed 2 of 2 + 2 ap

wanderer above the sea of fog 1818, 2015
cast aluminum
94 x 45 x 5 cm
ap 1 of 2 + ed of 2

the evening 1822, 2016
bronze
94 x 45 x 4 cm
ed 1 of 2 + 2 ap

two men by the sea 1817, 2021
bronze
56 x 46 x 4 cm
ed 1 of 2 + 2 ap

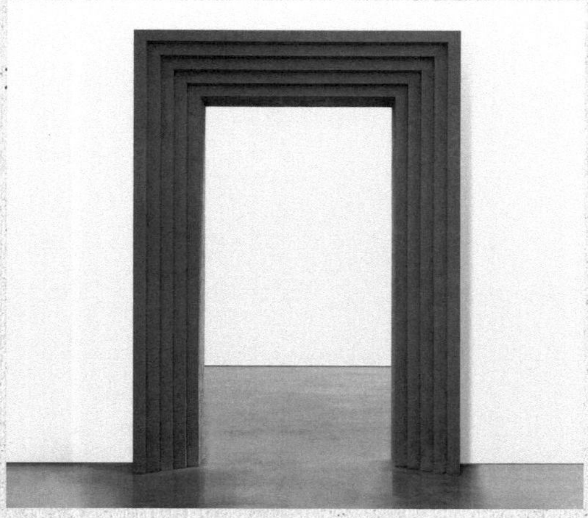

the golden presence, 2021
faux concrete and wood
401 x 275 x 50 cm

biography

ugo rondinone

1964
born in brunnen, switzerland

1986–90
studied at the hochschule für angewandte kunst, vienna

lives and works in new york

solo exhibitions

2021
vocabulary of solitude, museo tamayo, mexico
nude in the landscape, belvedere 21, vienna
a low sun . golden mountains . fall, galerie krobath, vienna
waterfalls & clouds, two person show with pat steir, galerie eva presenhuber, zürich
sail me on a silver sun, the national exemplar, iowa city
still.life., journal gallery, new york
your age and my age and the age of the rainbow, belvedere, vienna
a rainbow . a nude . bright light . summer, kamel mennour, paris
a yellow a brown and a blue candle, the national exemplar, iowa city
nuns + monks, gladstone gallery, new york
chuck nanney + joel otterson, curated by ugo rondinone, martos gallery, new york
ned smyth — life, curated by ugo rondinone, the landcraft garden, mattituck
a sky . a sea . distant mountains . horses . spring ., sadie coles, london
feeling the void and the rhone, kunsthalle marcel duchamp, cully
a wall. a door. a tree. a lightbulb. winter, skmu sørlandets kunstmuseum, kristiansand

2020
the monk, sant'andrea de scaphis, rome
nuns + monks, esther schipper, berlin
nuns + monks, galerie eva presenhuber, zürich
poetry, two person show with john dilg, the national exemplar, iowa city

2019
medellín mountain, medellín modern art museum, colombia
thanx 4 nothing, gladstone gallery, new york
a wall . seven windows . four people . three trees . some clouds . one sun, kamel mennour, paris
everyone gets lighter, kunsthalle helsinki, finland
sunny days, guild hall, east hampton
thanx 4 nothing, carré d'art, chapelle des jésuites, nîmes
earthing, kukje gallery, seoul

2018
the true, laguna gloria, the contemporary austin
liverpool mountain, liverpool biennial, tate liverpool
clockwork for oracles, phillips, paris
the marciano collection, marciano foundation, los angeles
the radiant, malta international contemporary art space, valetta
drifting clouds, gladstone gallery, new york
your age and my age and the age of the sun, fundación casawabi, puerto escondido

2017
vocabulary of solitude, arken museum of modern art, ishøj
moonrise. east. july, aspen art museum, aspen
good evening beautiful blue, bass museum of art, miami

flower moon, bristol hotel, paris
where do we go from here, the istanbul biennial, istanbul
i love john giorno, various institutions, new york,
the sky over manhattan, sky art, new york,
the world just makes me laugh, berkeley art museum and pacific film archive, berkeley
let's start this day again, contemporary arts center, cincinnati
winter moon, maxxi, rome,
your age my age and the age of the rainbow, the garage museum of contemporary art, moscow

2016
every time the sun comes up, place vendôme, paris
two men contemplating the moon 1830, esther schipper, berlin
miami mountain, bass museum of art, miami
the sun at 4pm, gladstone gallery, new york
girono d'oro + notti d'argento, mercati dietraiano, rome
girono d'oro + notti d'argento, macro, rome
becoming soil, carré d'art, nîmes
seven magic mountains, art production fund and nevada museum of art / desert of nevada
vocabulary of solitude, boijmans van beuningen, rotterdam
primordial, gladstone gallery, brussels
ugo rondinone: moonrise sculptures, the institute of contemporary art (ica), boston
windows, poems, and stars, la caja negra, madrid

2015
i love john giorno, palais de tokyo, paris
mountains + clouds + waterfalls, sadie coles hq, london
feelings, kukje gallery, seoul
walls + windows + doors, galerie eva presenhuber, zürich
golden days and silver nights, art gallery of nsw, sydney
artists and poets, curated by ugo rondinone, secession, vienna
clouds, galerie krobath, vienna

2014
breathe walk die, rockbund art museum, shanghai
naturaleza humana, museo anahuacalli, coyoacán

2013
human nature, public art fund, rockefeller plaza, new york
we run through a desert on burning feet, all of us are glowing our faces look twisted, art institute of chicago, chicago
thank you silence, m museum, leuven
pure moonlight, almine rech gallery, paris
primal, esther schipper, berlin
soul, gladstone gallery, new york
soul, galerie eva presenhuber, zürich
primal, sommer contemporary art, tel aviv
poems, sorry we're closed, brussels
fatima center for contemporary culture, monterrey

2012
primitive, the common guild, glasgow
pure sunshine, sadie coles hq, london
nude, cycladic art museum, athens
wisdom?peace?blank?all of this?, kunsthistorisches museum, theseustempel, vienna
the moth poem and the holy forest, galerie krobath, vienna

2011
we are poems, gladstone gallery, brussels
new horizon, almine rech gallery, brussels
we are poems, lvmh, palais an der oper, munich
kiss now kill later, galerie eva presenhuber, zürich
we run through a desert on burning feet, all of us are glowing our faces look twisted, art basel, art parcours, basel
outside my window, peder lund, oslo

2010
nude, gladstone gallery, new york
ibm building, new york
turn back time. let's start this day again, fiac, hors les murs, jardins des tuileries, paris
clockwork for oracles, art basel, art unlimited, basel
sunrise. east, museum dhondt-dhaenens, deurle
die nacht aus blei, aargauer kunsthaus, aarau

2009
sunrise. east, festival d'automne à paris, jardin des tuileries, paris
how does it feel?, festival d'automne à paris, le 104, paris
nude, sadie coles hq, london
la vie silencieuse, galerie almine rech, paris
the night of lead, musac, museo de arte contemporáneo de castilla, léon

2008
clockwork for oracles ii, ica boston, art wall project, boston
turn back time. let's start this day again, galleria raucci/santamaria, naples
sunrise. east, frieze art fair, outdoor project, london
we burn, we shiver (with martin boyce), sculpture center, new york
moonrise. east, public art project, art basel, basel
twelve sunsets, twenty nine dawns, all in one, galerie eva presenhuber, zürich
dog days are over, hayward gallery, southbank centre, london

2007
big mind sky, matthew marks gallery, new york
wohnsiedlung werdweis, kunst und bau, zürich-altstetten
get up girl a sun is running the world (with urs fischer), church san stae, 52nd venice biennale, venice
our magic hour, arario gallery, cheonan

air gets into everything even nothing, creative time, ritz carlton plaza, battery park, new york

2006
giorni felici, galleria civica di modena, modena
on butterfly wings, galerie almine rech, paris
thank you silence, matthew marks gallery, new york
unday, galerie esther schipper, berlin
a waterlike still, ausstellungshalle zeitgenössische kunst, munster
my endless numbered days, sadie coles hq, london
zero built a nest in my navel, whitechapel gallery, london

2005
clockwork for oracles, isr-centro culturale svizzero di milano, milan
sunsetsunrise, sommer contemporary art, tel aviv

2004
sail me on a silver sun, galleria raucci/santamaria, naples
long gone sole, matthew marks gallery, new york
long night short years, le consortium, dijon
clockwork for oracles, australian centre for contemporary art, melbourne

2003
la criée, théâtre national de bretagne, galerie art & essai, rennes
moonrise, galerie hauser & wirth & presenhuber, zürich
our magic hour, museum of contemporary art, sydney
lessness, galerie almine rech, paris
roundelay, musée national d'art moderne, centre georges pompidou, paris

2002
in alto arte sui ponteggi, centro culturale svizzero, milan
our magic hour, centre for contemporary visual arts, brighton
coming up for air, württembergischer kunstverein, stuttgart
1988, works on paper inc., los angeles
lowland lullaby (with urs fischer), swiss institute, new york
cigarettesandwich, sadie coles hq, london
the dancer and the dance, galerie krobath wimmer, vienna
no how on, kunsthalle wien, vienna
a horse with no name, matthew marks gallery, new york
on perspective, galleri faurschou, copenhagen

2001
slow graffiti, galerie schipper & krome, berlin
frac paca, marseille
yesterday's dancer, sommer contemporary art, tel aviv
dreams and dramas, herzliya museum of contemporary art, herzliya
kiss tomorrow goodbye, palazzo delle esposizioni, rome
if there were anywhere but desert, galerie almine rech, paris

2000
so much water so close to home, moma p.s.1, new york
love invents us, matthew marks gallery, new york
if there were anywhere but desert, mont-blanc boutique, new york
a doubleday and a pastime, galleria raucci/santamaria, naples
in the sweet years remaining, aarhus art museum, aarhus
hell, yes!, sadie coles hq, london

1999
guided by voices, galerie für zeitgenössische kunst leipzig, leipzig
guided by voices, kunsthaus glarus, glarus
moonlighting, galerie hauser & wirth & presenhuber, zürich
light of fallen stars, yves saint-laurent, new york
in the sweet years remaining, schipper & krome, berlin

1998
in the sweet years remaining, galerie joão graça, lisbon
the evening passes like any other, galerie almine rech, paris
so much water so close to home, galerie krobath wimmer, vienna

1997
stillsmoking, galleria raucci/santamaria, naples
moonlight and aspirin, galleria bonomo, rome
tender places come from nothing, cato jans der raum, hamburg
where do we go from here, le consortium, dijon

1996
dog days are over, migros museum für gegenwartskunst, zürich
le case d'arte, milan
heyday, centre d'art contemporain, geneva

1995
meantime, galerie froment-putman, paris
migrateurs, arc – musée d'art moderne de la ville de paris, paris
cry me a river, galerie walcheturm, zürich

1994
galerie daniel buchholz, cologne
galerie six friedrich, munich

1993
drawings, centre d'art contemporain de martigny, martigny
lightyears, galerie ballgasse, vienna

1992
c, galerie walcheturm, zürich

1985 – 1991
far away trains passing by, galerie martina detterer, frankfurt
two stones in my pocket, galerie pinx, vienna
i'm a tree, galerie walcheturm, zürich
galerie pinx, vienna
raum für aktuelle schweizer kunst, lucerne
sec 52, ricco bilger, zürich
galerie marlene frei, zürich